Courageous Faith

HOW TO RISE AND RESIST
IN A TIME OF FEAR

Emily C. Heath

THE PILGRIM PRESS

CLEVELAND

In memory of
SAMMY,
who taught me that faith
is resistance.

For
CAROL,
who taught me that
hope is resistance,
and

for
HEIDI,
who teaches me every
day that love is resistance.

The Pilgrim Press, 700 Prospect Avenue, Cleveland, Ohio 44115
thepilgrimpress.com
© 2017 by Emily C. Heath

Scripture quotations, unless otherwise noted, are from the New Revised
Standard Version of the Bible, © 1989 by the Division of Christian Education
of the National Council of the Churches of Christ in the United States
of America, and are used by permission. Changes have been made for
inclusivity.

Printed in the United States of America on acid-free paper

21   20   19   5   4   3   2

ISBN 978-0-8298-2039-3

CONTENTS

Acknowledgments

Once again I am profoundly grateful to everyone who supported me in the process of writing this book. Too many people to name helped me to think through the ideas behind this book and then supported me as it came to life. There are a few to whom I am particularly grateful, though.

In particular, I am thankful for Tina Villa and the whole team at the Pilgrim Press. After they published my first book, they believed that this second book had a place with them as well. Their support would be a gift to any writer.

I am especially grateful to the Congregational Church in Exeter (UCC). They always support my writing, and they encourage me to share my thoughts with the wider church. My first call is always to be their pastor, and I give thanks every day for that gift.

I also hold in my heart a special place for those who have been fellow companions on the journey of recovery. Much of what they have taught me is found in this book, and I am profoundly grateful.

My friends and family have blessed me with wisdom and humor at every turn and have been tremendous sources of strength. The abundance of love that I receive from them is more than sufficient proof to me of God's grace.

Finally, the Rev. Heidi Carrington Heath is my partner and equal in both marriage and ministry. From the very first moments of her life, quite literally, she fought to live. Today she thrives and epitomizes what it means to be a survivor. She also does this with integrity, courage, and more than a little style. Thank you, Heidi, for your love and for always being my first reader.

Prologue | IN THE TOMBS

WHAT WOULD I HAVE DONE?

There are times that require people of faith to become people of courage.

Knowing full well the danger, Martin Luther stands before the Diet of Worms and stands behind his 95 Theses. Dietrich Bonhoeffer boards a ship back to Nazi Germany, leaving the safety of a teaching job in the United States behind, and joins the resistance. Rosa Parks looks up from her bus seat and tells the drier she won't be moving today. Martin Luther King Jr. walks across the Pettus Bridge in Selma, Alabama, and meets the violence of billy clubs and police dogs. Oscar Romero kneels at the altar as death squads enter the church.

In each of these moments a person of faith summons up courage alongside their fear and sets themselves on a path from which there is no turning back. They effect change that ripples far out beyond themselves, transforming their time and place. Today we look at their actions, hold them up as examples of faithful action, and proclaim that this is what it means to be a true follower of Christ.

I believe that is true. I also know that the biggest question of my life has always been this: "In a time of deep moral crisis, would I have done the right thing?" We all want to believe that we would have, but without living through a time of challenge, how do we really know? It's easy to hear stories from the past and say, "I would have stood up. I would have been courageous." Until we ourselves are tested, though, we will never know.

My mother gave me a copy of Anne Frank's *The Diary of a Young Girl* when I was still in elementary school. As I read the book I began to wonder, "Would I have hidden Anne's family?" "Would I have stood up to the Nazis?" What bothered me was the fear that I would have become one of the crowd, comfortably assured by the fact that I was in the majority and, therefore, in the eyes of my friends, in the right. I wondered about the ordinary people living in places where injustice had reigned supreme. Why had they stood by and let it happen? Surely they weren't all evil sociopaths? Why had they not stopped it? Why hadn't they resisted?

I think these questions had a hand in my own journey of faith. When I began my own Christian journey in earnest, at age seventeen, I was intrigued by the story of Jesus, who I believe to be God incarnate. Jesus was killed not by fringe extremists, but by completely legal means and with popular support. I was struck by the fact that in his final hours he was betrayed by one disciple and abandoned by all the rest.

What kind of faith was this? The leader, far from being a darling of the state, was arrested and executed. Meanwhile the "good guys" who formed his inner circle (let alone the bystanders who watched) were all too scared to do anything about it.

As time went on, though, I wondered whether maybe this was the point. Maybe in Jesus's life and death we are shown that our faith, in its authentic form at least, will rarely be popular or safe. Maybe we are taught that it will require a rare courage from us, one that not even the disciples could fully understand. In fact, until we can understand that, maybe we can never fully understand the improbability and power of resurrection.

COURAGE AND FEAR

This is a book about courage. It is also a book about fear. It cannot be one without the other because the two go hand in hand. Fear is natural, and it is not something to be avoided. It warns us when the stakes are high and we are in danger. It can be extraordinarily useful.

Franklin Roosevelt is famous for saying, "The only thing we have to fear is fear itself." The trouble with fear is not that it exists. The trouble, as Roosevelt well knew, was how our fear can control us and hold us back. Fear keeps us from doing what may be risky but is also right. In short, the problem with fear comes in the way we respond to it.

We often hear that when we are afraid we go into "fight or flight" mode. Most of us feel fear and choose "flight"; we get as far away from the thing that is threatening us as possible. The disciples did this on the night that Jesus was betrayed. Occasionally, though, we choose to "fight." We stand our ground and clench our fists, ready for the first punch, metaphorical or otherwise.

Scientists now tell us there's a third reaction too: freeze. Confronted with the enormity of a situation, and the potential for damage, we find ourselves immobilized and unable to react at all. In order to survive we blend in, seeking safety through inaction.

All three reactions are understandable. We all carry our histories with us into any interaction. Fear, memories of negative encounters, and even past traumas inform the way we act. The trouble is that these are reactions, not responses. Our body, led by the more reptilian parts of our brain, reacts to a perceived threat without really facing it.

In Christ we find another way. Christ teaches us not to react to the very real threats of the world, but to respond to them. In becoming incarnate, or human, God chose not to flee but to become one of us in the person of Jesus Christ. In his trial and crucifixion, Jesus did not take up arms to fight, nor did he urge his disciples to wage a war. Instead, throughout his ministry Jesus does not freeze, but remains on the move, intervening in matters of justice, putting himself in the middle of the struggles of the "least of these," healing the sick, and advocating for the forgotten and exiled.

By his life and death, Jesus gives us a new option: response, not reaction. By his example we are taught to be people of courage, choosing to engage when sometimes it is easier to run away, throw a punch, or fade into the background. In Jesus's resurrection we learn an even greater truth: by his courageous response to the world, and his radical participation in it, his death became not the end but rather the beginning of new life.

In short, resurrection is resistance. Resurrection is God's response to a world where injustice reigns so supreme that it would rather kill love and grace incarnate than welcome it. Resurrection is the final word to a culture of death, a refusal to allow goodness and mercy to be buried. Christians are called to be people of resurrection whose work is to respond to this broken world and to proclaim new life to those in need of hope.

This is especially true in times of deep moral crisis. These are the moments when Christians are given the chance to discover whether they really would stand up to oppression and injustice. Deeply confusing, these moments require us to reject the larger cultural narrative that everything is fine and to listen instead to the gospel of Jesus. These are the days that require a moral courage that is uncommon and that must be cultivated carefully.

I believe that we, the church, are facing one of these times.

We live in an era of confusion. Truth has been willfully obscured, and we are distracted by accusations of "fake news." Advances in civil rights and inclusion are being backpedaled. International relations are jeopardized, and the possibility of new armed conflicts loom on the horizon. Dissent, far from a foundation upon which reasonable civilizations depend, is now seen as disloyal at best and criminal at worst.

In the baptismal vows of my own tradition, which are similar to those of most other Christian churches, the baptismal candidate (or their parent) is asked this question: "Do you promise, by the grace of God, to be Christ's disciple, to follow in the way of our Savior, to resist oppression and evil, to show love and justice, and to witness to the work and word of Jesus Christ as best you are able?" The answer is "I do."

Resistance is written right into our baptismal vows. Our job as Christians is to resist anything that would strip any of God's beloved children of their full humanity. This is not a matter of partisan politics, nor a matter of whom you vote for at the polls. (Here it is worth noting that the proposal for this book predated the resistance movement following the 2016 American elections, though some may find resonance between the two.) Instead, this is about turning reigning structures and systems on their head by reforming them and telling the world that there is a better way.

The catch is that resisting the oppression and evil of the world, and instead following Christ, requires us first to resist our own reactive fear. Only by learning how to do so may we ever develop any kind of lasting moral courage. Learning to resist fear and to live into the hope of the resurrection is not easy. In fact, it is deeply personally challenging. Before we can confront and change the world, though, we must first dare to confront and change ourselves.

BEFORE RESURRECTION

In the pages that follow we will explore how to cultivate the courage to resist fear. Fear and courage are not opposed to one another. One must not eradicate fear completely in order to demonstrate courage. In fact, to feel no fear would be a sign that something was seriously wrong. Instead, this book is about resisting the ways in which unexamined fear keeps us from being courageous and choosing to respond courageously to the world.

I sometimes remind my congregation that the original Easter Sunday was not one of joy and celebration. There was no brass section playing "Jesus Christ Is Risen Today," no flowered cross, and no Easter egg hunt. Instead, there were the people who loved Jesus most, filled with grief, trudging toward his grave. When they arrived their grief was only increased when they found that it was empty and that Jesus was nowhere to be found.

We have the benefit of knowing how this story ends. We know that Jesus suffered the worst that the world could do to him, was destroyed by it, and then rose up again for us all. Resurrection, God's promise of new life to us, is the point of our Christian faith. Resurrection is glorious and joyful! Eventually. That's because resurrection only comes not just after the cross but also after the tombs. And too often we are scared to death to talk about the tombs.

We should talk about it, because we all spend some time in the tombs, whether we admit it or not. There's a strong possibility that you might be in the tombs yourself right now. The tombs of this life are not the places where we are literally dead, but instead the areas where we are stuck while we are waiting to fully live. They are the places we are relegated to before we are able to fully claim the resurrection given to us all.

Some of the tombs we live in are of our own making. Others are imposed on us by the world. We live in tombs of greed and addiction, racism and homophobia, hatred of others and hatred of self, xenophobia and alienation, deceit and silence, and as many others as there are people on this earth. We are all in some way held back from full participation in the resurrection of Christ by the brokenness of a world that sometimes feels as joyful as a graveyard.

The good news is that we don't have to live like this. Jesus says in the Gospel of John that "the thief comes only to steal and kill and destroy. I came that they may have life, and have it abundantly" (John 10:10). Jesus does not want us to live our life in the tombs, but to resist the "thieves" of the world who attempt to steal life from us. He wants for us to share in the resurrection, not just by living, but by living fully.

Jesus also makes clear that we should not just enjoy this fullness of our own lives, but share it with others. The greatest commandment includes the guidance that we should "love our neighbors as ourselves" (Matt. 22:36–40). For those of us who are able to find our way out of the tombs, that means stepping back and helping others to see the light as well. This need to claim resurrection, not just for ourselves but for the world, is why courage matters.

That's a tall order, but, thankfully, we are not asked to do anything that Jesus has not already done. There is a story from the television show *The West Wing*. A younger staffer, who is struggling with post-traumatic stress disorder, fears that he might risk his job if he gets the treatment he needs. He goes to the president's chief-of-staff, a recovering alcoholic, who tells him a story about a hole and a man who falls in it.

The man is out walking and falls down in hole. He finds himself at the bottom, and, no matter what he tries, he can't climb out. So he begins to call out for help. First a doctor walks by and, stopping briefly, writes the man a prescription and throws it down to the man before walking away. Next a clergy person walks by and, answering the man's calls for help, says a prayer for him before continuing on their way. But finally a friend walks by and, seeing the man at the bottom of the hole, the friend jumps in.

The man looks at his friend incredulously and asks, "What are you doing?! Now we're both stuck down here!"

"Yes," says the man. "But I've been here before, and I know the way out."[1]

The most beautiful thing about the incarnation, of God becoming one of us in the form of Jesus Christ, is that God jumps down into the hole with us. God knows what it is like to live in the tombs, and God knows how to get us out. Resurrection is not an academic exercise for Christians. Resurrection is following Jesus out of the tomb and into new life. It is with this assurance of resurrection that we can begin the work of resisting fear and claiming new life.

THE COURAGE TO CHANGE

This book is broken into two sections. The first is "Rise: The Courage to Change Our Lives," which is focused on recovery. The second is "Resist: The Courage to Change the World," which is focused on living in, and sharing resurrection with, all of God's creation. Within each of those sections are six chapters, for a total of twelve. Every chapter's title consists of one word, each of which points to a quality that is needed in order for people of faith to move from a place of fear to one of courageous action.

Before turning to the chapters, I want to share more with you about how they came to be in this order. In writing this book I was tempted to skip straight to part II, which is most focused on doing generative work in the larger world. As stated earlier, I believe we are in a time that requires great moral courage and Christian action. When time feels at a premium, reacting quickly to the situation at hand may feel like the clear course of action.

I've been working for social justice for my entire adult life, though, and I've also been around churches. I have observed the price that is sometimes paid when we rush into the next big battle without first doing the work of healing ourselves. Burnout in both communities of faith and activist communities is high. After operating in "fight" mode for so long, people wear down easily. In churches committed to transformative work, too often members come, engage quickly, assume leadership roles, grow tired and frustrated, and leave.

I have wrestled with that pattern myself. I came out as gay in the South in 1994, long before the social acceptance of LGBTQ people was anywhere close to where it is now. I committed myself to the work of justice. But, like many others, I burned out by my late twenties. In the aftermath I began to look for the reason why, and for a better way.

I started by thinking about people I knew who were able to both create real change in the world and also remain engaged and fulfilled. These were people who did not deny the brokenness or the unfairness around them, but who also created lives of meaning, and even joy. Many of these leaders were survivors, recovering from every sort of pain imaginable. And yet, they seemed to draw wisdom from the broken roads they had traveled, and to thrive, at least in part, because of what they had learned on that journey.

The more I studied the lives of the leaders, one common component of their stories kept coming up: before they had acquired the courage to change the world, each of them had first wrestled with finding the courage to change their own lives. It was this realization that convinced me that any would-be change agents of the world must first have the courage to reflect on their own lives, and be transformed. We cannot hope to bring new life to others if we refuse to seek it for ourselves. As Jesus once said, "Physician, heal yourself (Luke 4:23)." The process of becoming courageous enough to change this world begins internally.

WHO AND WHOSE WE ARE

As I studied the lives of leaders, the work of psychiatrist Erik Erikson began to resonate with me. Erikson's theories on psychosocial development sought to explain the work of the human life cycle. Erikson argued that there are nine stages to our lives. The three that interest me the most are the fifth through seventh, which deal with "fidelity," "love," and "care," and which cover adolescence, early adulthood, and adulthood.[2]

Erikson believed that the "fidelity" stage is when we explore our own identity, figuring out who we are and what values guide us. The "love" stage is when we learn about intimacy, how to love, and how to not be isolated in the world. Finally, the "care" stage is when we do what Erikson called the "generative" work of our lives. This is when we are able to create new things, work for justice, and find our purpose and calling.

Feminist scholars have rightfully pointed out that Erikson's framework works for men, particularly those who have cultural privilege because of their race, economic status, sexual orientation, and other factors. For many of us, though, this work takes place at different times in the lifespan. The work of identity, for instance, might not be completed in adolescence by someone who is facing societal pressures to conform to a different identity, such as a gay man.

Despite different understandings of timing, though, I do agree with Erikson's idea that before we can really do constructive and generative work in the world, particularly if we want to sustain this work over the long run, we have to figure out some things about ourselves and about how we relate to God and others. This is the work of identity and intimacy, and it's work that we sometimes overlook as people of faith, especially in the mainline and progressive churches where cultivating disciples is too often seen as unimportant.[3]

Bob Pazmino, a professor of Christian education at Andover Newton Theological School, argues that Christians must do the work of figuring out "who and whose we are" first before doing other work. In other words, we must do "identity" and "intimacy" work. For Pazmino, our identity work must be deeply internally reflective, and our intimacy work must stem from our knowledge that "whose we are" is God's.[4]

When we are able to do this work, we find that not only are we more integrated and healthy, but we are able to create healthier communities and to work to form a healthier world. Without these foundations, our work is rootless, and we become brittle and prone to burnout. At best, we are ineffective. At worst, we become reckless and dangerous. That is why, while we may feel in a rush to become generative, it is imperative to start with the life-changing work of identity and intimacy that is contained in the first section of this book.

RISE AND RESIST

In this book we will be on a resurrection journey. In part I, "Rise," we will focus on what it means to begin to claim resurrection by using principles from recovery communities. I have chosen the recovery community because this is a place where everyday people cultivate the courage to resist fear and find new life. Using these principles we will explore what it means to climb out of the tombs and into the light. This is the formative work of identity and intimacy that Erikson advocates.

In part II, "Resist," we will look at what it means to resist and to embody resurrection by how we live in the world. To live resurrection is to resist our fear of the destructive powers of the world and to move into the work of creating real and sustaining change. This is the generative work that depends upon the foundational recovery work of part I. Strengthened by our own work of healing, we will explore what it means to courageously engage in the work of disrupting patterns of oppression and creating a different way.

In both sections you will confront fear and commit to change, sometimes in yourself and sometimes in the world. This is the hard work, and liberating work, of moving aside the stones that block your way out of the tomb. As you do this work, give yourself time and space to go as slowly as you need, knowing that you are doing the work of clearing a path to new life for yourself.

As we begin, I offer this. At the conclusion of my previous book, I told the story of Nachshon. When Moses and company fled the oppressive pharoah, the armies of Egypt in close pursuit, they came to the edge of the Red Sea. With the waters in front of them, and certain death behind, they needed a miracle. In most retellings of the story that miracle takes place when Moses raises his arms and commands the waters to part, which quickly and neatly they do, leaving a clear and dry path through the middle.

Midrashic tradition, handed down over millennia by rabbis, teaches that it may not have happened quite like that. Instead, in the moment of greatest fear and crisis, God told Moses to tell the people to move forward. Seeing nothing but an unknown sea, no one dared to take the first step. That's when Nachshon enters the story. Stepping down the bank, he stuck a foot in the water, and it parted just a little bit. Then, taking the next step, the water parted a little more. Step by step, little by little, the water receded, and the people were saved.

I told that story one Sunday from the pulpit, hoping that no one was there to correct my pronunciation of "Nachshon." As luck, or grace, would have it, a rabbi happened to be sitting in the pews that day, there to witness the baptism of a friend's child. After worship I approached her, and asked if I'd been faithful to the story. Her answer? "Almost."

The rabbi told me that Nachshon's name should always be pronounced with a hard "ch" sound in the throat. It should feel almost like you are choking. The reason is that tradition teaches that the waters did not begin to part for Nachshon as soon as he dipped a toe in. Instead, he took a first step, and then another, and another. It wasn't until the waters rose up past his waist, over his shoulders, and covered his nose and mouth that they began to give way. It took almost drowning before things started to change.

The name Nachshon has come to mean "initiator." A "Nachshon" is someone who will risk taking the first step, and going even deeper, before anyone else. A "Nachshon" is also someone who will put themselves on the line in order to bring liberation to everyone else. In short, a "Nachshon" is someone who will resist fear and choose a path of courage in a time of moral crisis.

The work at hand cannot be done while standing on the water's edge. It can't even be done by occasionally daring to dip a toe in the water. It can only be done by people who dare to be "all in," to immerse themselves in the work of bringing resurrection to themselves and to the world.

We are standing on the shore, and all the forces of modern-day pharaohs are bearing down upon us. In front of us is a deep, churning sea. The journey through the waters will not be easy. We will have to step out in faith, despite our fear. To stand on the shore and wait for the alternative, though, is to risk the destruction of the image of God in us all. Standing still is no longer an option. The waters await us.

PART ONE

Rise

The Courage to Change Our Lives

ONE | READY

WHEN SOMETHING'S WRONG

On a snowy southern morning many years ago I parked my car behind a big white building. I'd woken up feeling sick. My stomach churned, my heart raced, and my mouth felt dry. But that wasn't the worst of it. That morning I had stumbled into the shower dry heaving, feeling like I was going to collapse. I couldn't look at myself in the mirror. I knew I couldn't do this anymore.

My freshman year of college I'd fallen in love . . . with alcohol. A few beers made an introverted kid feel comfortable at parties, and a couple of shots of whiskey made the stress of coming out as gay in the early 1990s South a little easier. By the end of my freshman year I'd gotten into trouble for underage drinking in the dorms. By the end of my sophomore year I was at a field party that was broken up by the police. By the time it was legal for me to drink, I already had a problem with alcohol. I knew, at some level, that my binge drinking wasn't normal. On the other hand, plenty of my college classmates were doing the exact same thing, if not worse.

I went off to seminary right after college. There I found plenty of others who would join me in overindulging. One of my most profound seminary memories is of getting drunk at the traditional party after we had taken our ordination exams. Another is of carrying a keg into the dorms the night before graduation. Then there was that time, a night before I was ordained, that a few college friends gave me an engraved silver flask reading "The Rev. Emily Heath." In retrospect, maybe that should have been a clue that there was a problem.

For the next few years I continued to drink. I didn't drink every day. I never drove drunk. I didn't drink at work. In many ways I never suffered any negative social or legal consequences for my drinking. Still, I was beginning to realize that something was wrong. Drinking had become my default way of dealing with depression, anxiety, societal homophobia, and the trauma that I was seeing daily as a pediatric emergency room chaplain.

I knew that I had a family propensity for addiction. My parents are not alcoholics, but a number of members of my family, for as many generations back as anyone can remember, have been what we would call "functional" alcoholics. My family has a tradition of military and government service, and family members held down jobs, often difficult ones involving great discretion, and stayed out of trouble. Inside the walls of their homes, though, their families lived with their addiction and all its consequences.

On that morning when I woke up from another night of drinking, I knew I was at a crossroads. I could choose to keep up the family tradition and self-medicate my way through life. Or I could claim a little bit of resurrection, and I could get help.

More than a decade later, each day of which had been spent without a drink, I would try to remember what that morning felt like. I would remember sitting in that parking lot, waiting for a meeting of others who, like me, had a problem. I didn't want to walk in the doors. I didn't want to admit there was a problem. I didn't want to utter the words that I had resisted saying for so long: "Hi, my name is Emily, and I'm an alcoholic."

Years later, I'm so glad I did anyway.

RECOVERY IS FOR EVERYONE

If you picked up this book to read about courage and resisting fear, you might be wondering why I'm telling you about my drinking. That's a fair question, but what I really want to tell you about has nothing to do with the details of my addiction. Instead I want to share the profound gifts and graces that I have found in recovery. It is recovery, sometimes even more than the church, that has taught me what it means to live a faithful and courageous life, and it is recovery that has given me the tools to do so.

The first section of this book deals with recovery principles. This is a journey that can teach us to resist fear and find new life. It may be tempting to skip this work and go straight to what is contained in later chapters. I'm asking you to bear with me, though, because it is this foundation that can transform us and strengthen us for the work to be done. Here we can develop tools that will help us to be reflective about ourselves and to persevere in our work. That's important because, if we really believe we are called to transform the world, this work is too important to do without preparing ourselves rigorously and well.

First, I want to acknowledge that you may not think you need recovery. Maybe you have never wrestled with an addiction or compulsion, or loved someone who has. Perhaps you believe that recovery is for the morally irresponsible, people whose choices have put them in the position of needing some sort of remedial help that they can only find in recovery meetings. You might feel a little like the proverbial brother of the prodigal son, wondering why such a fuss is being made about them while you've been here doing the right thing your entire life.

I get that. If this isn't something you think you need, that's okay. I'm asking you to read it as background anyway, because while you may not need grace in your life, I'll bet you know a lot of people who do. Perhaps this can help you to help them. Or, just maybe, you might even find something here for you. I believe you might, because I believe recovery is for everyone. You don't need to qualify for a twelve-step group to benefit from these ideas.

If we are honest with ourselves, though, I think we can all admit that we know what it's like to be in the proverbial tombs from time to time. As I said in the preface, there are a lot of tombs in this world, both of our own making and of society's. I have dwelt in the tomb of alcoholism, a tomb that I was in some ways genetically chosen for, but a tomb that was also of my own making because of my own choices. But I have also spent too much time in the tomb of homophobia. Others have lived in tombs of racism, sexism, transphobia, classism, ableism, and more. These are not tombs we choose for ourselves. These are tombs that we are placed in through injustice, and too often told to stay there. It doesn't matter what tomb you are in, or how you got there. It just matters that you are ready to get out.

Recovery is about refusing to stay in the tombs. Recovery is nothing less than lived resistance to the forces of fear and death. In recovery we learn to first identity our tombs and then, stone by stone, to clear away what is blocking our way out. In other words, in recovery we learn a lot about resurrection.

TAKE WHAT YOU NEED . . .

As we go deeper into this work it is important for me to tell you that, just as I am not a religious fundamentalist, I am far from a recovery fundamentalist. There are some who read the Big Book of Alcoholics Anonymous (the closest thing the recovery community has to scripture) as literally as a fundamentalist Christian reads the Bible. The words contained in the Big Book were written in 1939, mostly by

Bill Wilson, the founder of AA. It has not been modified since that time, except to include an appendix of updated personal stories with each new edition. Reading the Big Book sometimes feels like stepping back in time.

The twelve steps, too, though certainly life-saving for many, have also never been updated or changed. God is referred to in strictly masculine terms, for instance, and the alcoholic is also assumed to be male. Other recovery traditions may also feel restrictive rather than liberating, and those who impose rigid interpretations on newcomers can sometimes do more harm that good.

If you are reading this book, you are likely someone with a mainline or progressive view of Christianity. I encourage you to apply that same level of nuance to the concepts of recovery. This is not a manual on the twelve steps, or a definitive overview of recovery, though those concepts do inspire it. If, after consideration, something doesn't fit with your own understanding of yourself or your faith, I encourage you to take inspiration from an old recovery slogan: "Take what you need and leave the rest." Recovery should give you the tools to live a better life, not more stones to block your way. With that said, it's time to start the journey for ourselves.

THE FIRST STEP

It's a sign of the power of recovery that the first of the twelve steps of Alcoholics Anonymous has become something of a joke. We use it as a quip when a friend talks about how they can't stop drinking coffee, or going golfing. We laugh and say, "You know, the first step is admitting that you have a problem."

Recovery programs like Alcoholics Anonymous, Narcotics Anonymous, Al-Anon, and others use a common set of twelve steps, originally written for recovering alcoholics but adapted for each fellowship. The first step of AA reads: We admitted we were powerless over alcohol —that our lives had become unmanageable. In other words, before you can start any of the next eleven steps, you have to be able to admit that something's wrong.

The "powerlessness" that the first step names is sometimes taken to mean that we have no control over our disease, and therefore no responsibility for addressing it. That's a misinterpretation, though. By saying we are "powerless" we admit that something wants to destroy our lives and put us in the tombs. By naming it we are saying that we cannot, and will not, allow it to make our lives unmanageable anymore.

Denial is our biggest stumbling block. It is in many ways the biggest and most deadly of all stones in our path. It does not want to be moved. It wants us to trip over it and to stay put. Denial is what allows us to resist taking the first step. It tells us that things aren't really all that bad. It keeps us from stepping down into the waters of the Red Sea when the Egyptian army is bearing down on our backs.

When we admit that we are broken and that we need help, we are far from powerless. We are saying that we refuse to be powerless any longer. Denial is the killer of courage, but admitting that something is wrong is the start of every act of resistance that we can imagine. If we can't admit that there is a problem, we will never get to the point of resurrection. Moreover, until we are willing to be internally courageous, we cannot hope to be externally courageous.

This first step is sometimes the most difficult of all. To admit that things are not as they seem, that we have been wounded, or that we don't quite have it all together can be earth shattering. This is sometimes especially true for people of faith. We think we have to stay positive and happy. Sometimes we even enable others to continue destructive behavior because we are addicted to being "nice." The reality is that denial, our own and that of our communities, is lethal. Christians who are in denial about our own brokenness and convinced of our righteousness have the capacity to wreak havoc on an epic scale.

CHANGING AT ROCK BOTTOM

J. K. Rowling once spoke to a graduating Harvard class about the brokenness of her life before she was published. She was destitute, living on government assistance, unemployed, newly divorced with a small child, and deeply depressed. In the midst of this crisis, she began to write the Harry Potter series. "I was set free, because my greatest fear had already been realized, and I was still alive, " said Rowling. "Rock bottom became the solid foundation on which I rebuilt my life."[5]

Jesus was once telling his disciples about two men who built houses. One built on sand. When the rain and wind raged the house couldn't withstand it, and it fell. "And," says Jesus, "great was its fall!" By contrast, the other man built his house on rock. No matter how much rain or wind came, that house stood strong, because it had been built on rock (Matt. 7:24–27).

The greatest gift sobriety gave to me was knocking down my house. In admitting that my life had become unmanageable, I was able to get honest about the parts of my life that had been built on sand. Dismantling those parts of the house was painful and frustrating at times. Rebuilding them was challenging. In the end, like Rowling, I found that the solid foundation of rock bottom, the bedrock of God's love and grace, became the anchor of my being.

When denial keeps us from seeing that our houses are built on sand, we become convinced that we do not need to change anything. When we are shaken by the winds and rain of reality, though, that crisis can convince us to rebuild on solid ground. That kind of rebuilding and change is not easy, but it is life saving. In recovery we call our rock bottom moments "the gift of desperation." Things are so bad that we are ready to try something new. We are ready to change.

In that spirit, we often repeat a prayer said to be written by Reinhold Niebuhr: "God, grant me the serenity to accept the things I cannot change, courage to change the things I can, and the wisdom to know the difference." You may know this as the "Serenity Prayer" for its emphasis on acceptance and peace of mind. I've heard it argued, though, that it's really the "Change Prayer."

Serenity allows us to accept what we are "powerless" over in our lives. That acceptance is not the same as a reluctance to work for change. Instead, it's a form of acknowledgment. We acknowledge that something is broken, that the world is not as it should be, that our lives are harder than we hoped, and that there are some things that are beyond our immediate control. We cannot reverse history, for instance. To accept something is the opposite of denying it; we name it, acknowledge it, and make it real.

That's just the beginning, though. In the next line we ask for courage, specifically "courage to change the things I can." It is the courage to change that defines our recovery and our resistance. Acceptance of reality moves us from denial to a place where we really can take action, and all action is a form of change, and all change requires courage.

First, change requires the courage to admit that things are bad enough that we are ready to try something different. The morning I decided to get sober took some amount of courage. I could have remained in denial, believing that my life had not "become unmanageable." It's likely that I could have functioned at a high level for some time afterward. In admitting that I could not control my addiction, though, I was forced to ask myself a hard question: "What are you willing to do in order to make things better?"

Though I didn't know it at the time, I had faced the same quandary earlier in my life. When I first came out I had to wrestle mightily with the fact that there were some things I could not change about the world. I could not change the homophobia and heterosexism of history. I could not control what others thought of me when I walked down the street. I could not control the fact that I would sometimes be discriminated against because of who I was. I did not have to accept that this was right, but I did have to accept the reality of the situation in order to understand it.

What I could not accept was that I had no power to change things. To deny the existence of injustice is problematic, but to throw up one's hands and say, "Well, there's nothing I can do about it" is equally damaging. It's the equivalent of an alcoholic saying, "I have this disease, so I might as well drink myself to death." Denial and defeat are very different, but they are equally deadly.

Accepting myself as gay and coming out meant embracing the courage to change not myself, but the world. Becoming involved in LGBTQ groups, marching in Pride parades, lobbying politicians, and educating peers became positive responses to the injustice of the world. I could not change the past, but I could help to change the present conversation and shape the future. This work was sometimes not easy, and it often required relying on God-given courage, but it was far better than the alternative of hiding in silence and fearfully refusing to engage.

In the last line of the Serenity Prayer we ask for "wisdom to know the difference" between what we can and cannot change. While there are certainly always factors beyond our control, I would argue that most things can be changed if we only have the courage. Addictions, unimaginably powerful and all encompassing, are overcome. The entrenched homophobia of the mid-1990s, while still being eroded, has changed enough twenty years later that same-sex couples have the legal right to marry.

The impossible becomes just a matter of time when courageous people embrace the call to foster change. Wisdom comes in knowing that we are not powerless over our choice to respond to whatever we face. By admitting to ourselves that we are ready for things to change, we choose a path that requires exceptional courage. The good news is that we are never alone.

IN THE BELLY OF THE WHALE

God once told a young man named Jonah to go to the city of Nineveh, known for its great immorality and injustice, and to warn them to change their ways.

Jonah isn't on board with this plan. He's the kind of guy who doesn't rock the boat, and he prefers to stay close to home. The far-off city of Nineveh, with it terrible reputation, holds no appeal. So Jonah does the only logical thing: he runs away.

The trouble with running from God, though, is there's no place to go. Jonah flees on a ship but God sends a storm so strong that the other sailors begin to suspect Jonah is bad luck. Jonah himself confirms this and tells them to throw him overboard, which they eventually do. Jonah falls into the water, to what seems a certain death. Instead, a large fish (sometimes called a whale) swallows him, and for three days Jonah lives inside the fish's belly, praying to God and asking for mercy.

Jonah is as good as dead, deep in the tomb of a fish's stomach. He has hit rock bottom. He is stuck in the whale of denial. It is only when he can no longer run that he admits he needs God and asks for help, and it is only then that God has the fish spit him out onto dry land.[6]

Our resistance to God's love and grace is what gets us stuck. In denial, we run from God believing we can find another way. Exhausted, we languish in tombs, half dead, refusing to trust God. It is only when we open ourselves up to God's mercy that we find ourselves back on dry land, even if it is in Nineveh, the one place we didn't want to go to in the first place. It is only when we get to rock bottom, our own whale's belly, that we stop running and agree that anything, even Nineveh, is better than this.

RUNNING TOWARD GOD

In recovery, after the first step of admitting there is a problem, the second and third steps focus on admitting to God that we need help.[7] Step two reads that we "came to believe that a Power greater than ourselves could restore us to sanity." Step three reads "Made a decision to turn our will and our lives over to the care of God as we understood [God]."[8]

I had been a Christian, and an ordained minister at that, before I entered recovery. Steps two and three seemed redundant. At my ordination I had knelt before family and friends and committed myself to a life of service to the Gospel. Hadn't I already proven that I believed in God and had turned my life over to God? Why did I have to do it again?

In my first year of recovery I learned that my spiritual journey until that point had been an earnest one, but too often a fearful one. I loved God deeply, but I often didn't trust God. I was very good at standing on the shores and dipping a foot in, but less skilled at immersing myself in the waters and trusting that God would guide me. In other words, my spiritual life lacked courage.

That's a reason that recovery is at the beginning of this book. Before we can change the larger world we must, as Pazmino says, know "who and whose we are," and like Erikson says, we must do the work of knowing ourselves and loving others. This is the heart of recovery. We come to know that we are God's beloved and that we are created to love. Until we know this at the bedrock of our being, until we can do the work of healing, we cannot as Christians hope to have the courage necessary to love the world into change.

Fear makes us run away from God, looking for places we can hide. Recovery is about running toward God and finding our identity in God's redemption. In recovery we admit that we alone cannot save ourselves, an extremely countercultural idea, especially for many North American Christians. We need help, and it must come from something greater than us. Even if our faith is tenuous, we claim the words of the father who asked Jesus to heal his son, crying out, "I believe; help my unbelief" (Mark 9:23–25). We trust enough to step down off the bank and into the deep end, because openness to God will always mean openness to risk and to change.

In the first three steps we begin to develop a moral courage that prepares us for the work ahead. We learn to resist the strange attraction of denial and choose instead to be unsettled by the truth. We stop running, and we turn to God for help. We dare to wade into the deeper waters of faith knowing that, somehow, new life awaits us there. This is a process of personal transformation, and it is not optional for those who want to transform the world.

Courage will be required from all of us for the work ahead. We all have a Nineveh, a place we do not want to go, but that we cannot avoid forever. For many of us, that Nineveh is internal. Rather than face what is in us, we run from God and from ourselves. It is Nineveh that we are heading to in the next chapters, and so we will need courage. We just may find, though, that like Jonah we can move out of the places of death, and back into the light.

TWO | HONEST

BURYING THE TRUTH . . . SOMETIMES LITERALLY

Several years ago I was researching my family history. I was focusing on my great-great-grandparents, Alvah and Katie, who lived not far from where I do now. Alvah was the son of a New England Yankee family of long lineage. Katie was the daughter of Irish Catholic immigrants who had disowned her for marrying a Protestant. I knew their marriage was a minor rebellion, which made me smile a bit as I pulled up their marriage record, dated 1895, and added it to my family tree. But then, I saw something else.

Among the "marriage and divorce" records of the state of New Hampshire was another entry for that same couple, dated 1917. I pulled it up and was stunned to find that it was a divorce decree. I had certainly never heard of any divorces in older generations of my family. I had even been to the graves of this couple where they are buried side by side as husband and wife. Surely this was a mistake.

But it wasn't. There in print was Katie's petition to divorce Alvah, with this as the given reason why: "habitual drunkeness." Further research revealed to me that Alvah had wrestled with what today would be seen as serious alcoholism. He had been in and out of the county jail, seemingly unable to stay sober. Finally his long-suffering wife had enough. Katie divorced him and then, being estranged from her Catholic family, she died destitute and heartbroken only months later at the county poorhouse.

I asked my mother if she knew this story. She had never heard it. Her father, Katie and Alvah's grandson, would have been a child living in the same town at the time. Wouldn't he have known? If so, he never told anyone. We were left baffled. And then we found another record.

This time I was going through death and burial records. I found Katie's death certificate from 1917, and a record of her burial. Next I found Alvah's death certificate from 1928, and his own burial. And then I found the record that explained how none of us had known a thing. It was from 1928, and it was for the disinterment of Katie's body and the movement of her grave to a space right next to her ex-husband, Alvah's. The name at the bottom of the certificate authorizing the transfer? Their own daughter's—my great-grandmother.

What I know of my great-grandmother is that she was a formidable woman. Despite her hardscrabble background, she was well connected in the city where the family lived. She was active in church circles and took special interest in the Women's Christian Temperance Union, a group that worked for Prohibition and a complete abstinence from drinking. The WCTU reached its peak in the 1920s and 1930s, right about the time Alvah died after a lifetime of hard drinking.

I can't be sure exactly what was running through her head when she decided to disinter her mother and bury her with her estranged ex-husband, but I think the action was probably driven by shame. Divorce was uncommon in the early twentieth century, and even an adult child of divorce likely felt ashamed. Being a WCTU diehard whose father couldn't stop drinking was probably something she wanted to hide as well. Having a mother who was left to the mercy of the poorhouse after leaving a "drunk" must have been humiliating for the entire family.

So, if there was a way to create a little revisionist history, something for both her present-day friends and future generations, she may have reasoned, why not do it? Why not bury the bodies next to one another in the big city cemetery so that future generations could see that Alvah and Katie had ended up by one another's side even in death? When I had stood at the foot of Katie and Alvah's graves, after all, I had never thought that anything else was true. I never had reason to.

AS SICK AS OUR SECRETS

In writing this family story nearly one hundred years later, I confess to some trepidation. My great-grandmother went to great lengths to hide a family secret, and here I am writing it down in a book. Am I betraying her? Am I being disloyal? Some would certainly say "yes." Right now there's even a part of me that says "yes."

I'm choosing to tell this story anyway. This is a story of my family, one that was hidden from me and from other generations, probably with the belief that we would never find out. How could my great-grandmother have imagined the internet, which would allow us to pull up state archives from our living rooms, after all? But I did find it, and it has become my story because it has told me something about how we have in the past dealt with uncomfortable truths.

I am telling it here because I refuse to carry the burden of secrecy, especially when secrecy is not needed. In recovery we have a saying: "We're as sick as our secrets." When I heard that for the first time it struck a nerve. Recovery teaches us that secrecy can be an ideal breeding ground for addiction and disorder. What we hide from others and, more importantly, from ourselves can be what leaves us isolated and looking for ways to self-medicate away the pain.

As an example, take alcohol use and LGBTQ people. Alcohol abuse in the LGBTQ community has been estimated to be as high as

25 percent.[9] That rate may be slowly changing as newer generations come of age in a more accepting society, but it's not hard to see a connection between the pressures to remain "in the closet," hiding one's sexual orientation or gender identity, and the need to find a way to deal with the pain and isolation of hiding one's self.

Add to that the fact that coming out, even to yourself, is incredibly stressful. The homophobia and transphobia of society function to silence us. We may know at some level that we are LGBTQ, but no one can deny that it is still easier to be straight and gender conforming. For that reason, many LGBTQ people refuse to admit even to themselves that they might be gay or trans. Societal pressures are so effective that sometimes we even turn the violence inward, which is why suicide rates have always been high among gay, and particularly trans, youth.

There is still so much work to be done, but the increasing number of LGBTQ people who feel safe coming out has done much to increase visibility and to provide examples of healthy and thriving out people to younger generations. Being openly gay or trans, unthinkable in my high school only a couple of decades ago, is now not a big deal to many youth. (My own youth group finds it unthinkable that I waited until college to come out. I explain to them that at the time that was considered incredibly early.)

What the LGBTQ community teaches us about secrecy is that it can literally kill us. Having to deny who we are on a daily basis is exhausting and poisonous to the soul. Holding a secret, especially one you cannot admit even to yourself, is much like carrying around a heavy weight that you cannot put down. Eventually, it will break you down, one way or another. This is not in any way a judgment on LGBTQ people who choose to remain closeted; this is a judgment on the culture that forces them to feel like it is their only choice.

Being forced to keep secrets can make us sick. We have probably all, at one time or another, carried a secret that was unhealthy for us to hold. Maybe it was something we did for which we thought others would reject us. I have heard so many people come into my office and say, "If people knew the real me, they wouldn't like me anymore." This is very rarely true, but we believe it anyway.

Sometimes secrets are inflicted on us by others. Those who have survived abuse, either as children or adults, often keep the secret out of fear that they will not be believed. Often their abuser told them just that, or told them the lie that they were somehow responsible for their own abuse. Abusers thrive on the silencing of the ones they attack. While it is every survivor's right to decide when and where to share their story, no survivor should ever be intimidated or forced into silence by others.

Or maybe the secrets are family secrets, like the one I told you at the chapter's beginning, that we know not to share with outsiders. Perhaps we keep them not because we want to but because a sense of family loyalty compels our silence. Sometimes the secrets die with us, and we miss a chance to help other generations know more of their own truth. That doesn't mean they lose their power, though. Recent research shows that the effects of trauma can even be unconsciously passed down through generations of families, maybe even changing our very DNA.

Regardless of how our secrets are handed to us, until we can find some peace with them, they will eat away at us. This is not to say that every person must reveal everything to everyone. Our stories are ours to tell, and we can choose how we do, or do not, share them. Unless we are willing to do the work of telling the truth to ourselves, though, there will be no healing, and without healing we cannot hope to do the work of helping others.

The stumbling blocks we must remove from our path at this point are whatever fears are keeping us from being self-reflective. Like denial in the last chapter, our fear of self-reflection blocks our way out of the tombs, trapping us in a place of death. When we dare to roll those stones away, though, we find a clear way forward toward resurrection.

In our self-searching we can discover who we are on a deeper level, becoming better advocates for ourselves and better allies to others. By failing to do this work, however, we can become unknowingly dangerous to others, taking up too much space, looking for healing or acclaim in the wrong places, and reenacting our trauma on others. This work benefits us greatly, but it also benefits others, because we are always interconnected with one another.

The work of this phase is courageous and sacred. It is to learn to tell the story of our lives, choosing reality over the attractive comfort of denial and the fear of truth. To be honest with one's self is also a necessary step. Until we are able to recognize truth and falsehood in our own lives, we will never be able to recognize, name, and respond to these things in the world. Until we can be honest, we cannot be free.

THE TRUTH WILL SET YOU FREE

In the Gospel of John, chapter 8, there is a story about Jesus and a woman who is about to be killed by religious authorities, who have found her guilty of adultery. Jesus interrupts the execution, challenging the gathered crowd to find one person who has not sinned and to let that person throw the first stone. Slowly, the crowd thins out, until only Jesus and the woman remain. With no one left, Jesus sends her home, saying "I don't condemn you. Now go and sin no more" (John 8:11).

Jesus leaves the woman and goes into the temple, and begins to teach the crowd, telling them, "And you shall know the truth, and the truth shall set you free" (John 8:32). We tend to love that quote in the church. People even love it outside of the church. (It's the motto of the Central Intelligence Agency, after all.) But taken out of context, the verse loses its power.

When Jesus tells the crowd that the truth shall make them free, they do not rejoice. Instead they ask Jesus, "When were we ever not?" The crowd believes itself to be free. There is nothing that they are chained to and nothing holding them back. This freedom Jesus promises is nice but unnecessary. But Jesus answers them, saying, "Everyone who commits sin is a slave to sin" (John 8:34).

Just as there was no one who could throw the first rock, there is no one who can claim perfection. We all need freedom, because none of us is perfect, and we all need liberation, because none of us can hope to free others if we are held captive. Admitting our imperfection, though, is frightening. It means telling the truth about what we carry with us every day.

I want to offer a word of caution here. I am using Jesus's words here about sin, but I am not in any way calling every secret or shame that we keep a result of our own sin. Often what we carry, like the memories of abuse or the effects of bigotry, is the result of the sins of others. If you are carrying injuries brought on by the sins of others, you are not responsible for that. You did nothing to deserve that.

Here I am pointing out that both the sinful things that we do and those that are done to us are capable of destroying us. I define sin here as that which separates us, or others, from God. This includes the systemic sin that many of us live with every day. To not name or acknowledge the powerful effects of this systemic sin is to be in some ways complicit in it. Like those who were listening to Jesus, if we think we are not in some ways held back by this, we deceive ourselves.

When I was getting sober, I had to take a hard look at my own behaviors and choices, and to choose to now live in a different way. I also had to look at some of what I had lived with, and come to understand how it had shaped me. What did it mean to grow up gay in the South in the late twentieth century? How had I absorbed the lessons of that time and place, and internalized them? How had the sins of homophobia and transphobia shaped the conditions of my addiction?

I could not blame the world for my addiction, but I could not pretend I had lived in a bubble either. The intersectionality of our lives means that our mistakes do not just affect us. We are shaped by our world, and we shape our world, for good or for ill. When we commit to doing the work of being honest with ourselves we take responsibility for our own actions, but we also look at the things beyond our control that have shaped us, too. Until we do both, we cannot hope to truly be set free.

HOW DID I BECOME ME?

The fourth of the twelve steps calls on us to "make a searching and fearless moral inventory of ourselves." There's a reason why many newcomers to twelve-step groups stumble on this step and leave. More than any other step, being "searching and fearless" requires moral courage, and that is never comfortable. It is, however, incredibly valuable. Discomfort is far from death, after all, and in this case discomfort can even be an indication that new life is emerging.

There's a popular twist on Jesus's words: "The truth will set you free, but first it will make you miserable." Anyone who has ever made a "searching and fearless moral inventory" of themselves would likely agree. The founders of AA didn't set up an exact way to do this, and methods vary widely, but many people work their fourth step by writing out a list of all the things that they are holding inside of themselves that bring them shame, anger, resentment, or pain.

I can attest that this is not easy and that it takes a lot of paper. It is, however, extremely cathartic. To take the things that have been hidden inside of us for so long and to physically allow them out is to take a step toward resurrection. It is to overcome our fear just enough to break the chains that bind us to our tombs.

The founders of AA, who were men (and all men) of their own time, and who all carried significant privilege in terms of race, economic ability, and more, saw step four as a way of listing one's sins and repenting. I'm not saying that you shouldn't do that if it works for you, but I believe that this process is broader than that. In many ways, step four is about telling our story thus far. We are asking ourselves the question, "How did I become me?"

In order to do this, we look at the past—our history and the history of the families, communities, and cultures that have shaped us —and we tell the truth about it, good, bad, and otherwise. We tell the truth about not just what we have done, but what has happened to us. We locate ourselves within a greater story, and we paint a picture of how we came to be the people who we are today, conscious of the ways our story shapes how we look at ourselves, and how we interact with the world.

This is necessary work in great part because it helps us to let go of shame and helplessness. During the 2016 election cycle a therapist named Richard Brouillette wrote an essay for the *New York Times* entitled "Why Therapists Should Talk Politics." Brouillette related stories about clients who were contending with economic fears that impacted their ability to thrive, such as remaining in job situations that were beyond being not ideal or feeling deep shame about the possibility of unemployment.

Brouillette decided that he was going to break a longtime taboo in his field and start talking to his clients about social inequality. He writes, "It is inherently therapeutic to help a person understand the injustice of his predicament, reflect on the question of his own agency, and take whatever action he sees fit. . . . You would be surprised how seldom it occurs to people that their problems are not their fault."[10]

What Brouillette highlights is the fact that each of us is shaped by society. While he is focusing here on economic inequality, this idea could be expanded to any discrimination we face, deprivation we survive, or trauma we endure. Brouillete argues that we must look at the whole picture, including what we have no control over and how we came to be who we are now.

Some might argue that Brouillette is enabling his clients to just make excuses about why their life is not going the way they hope. On the contrary, he is equipping them to do the work of self-liberation. By understanding the complex, intersectional nature of their lives, he is helping them to rewrite their own futures. He writes, "By focusing on fairness and justice, a patient may have a chance to find what has so frequently been lost: an ability to care for and stand up for herself. Guilt can be replaced with a clarifying anger, one that liberates a desire—and a demand—to thrive, to turn outward toward others rather than inward, one that draws her forward to make change."[11]

In any good reflective process, whether therapy or recovery or spiritual growth, we have to do the work of examining our lives. To do this work without looking at the family events and social forces that shaped us is to deny that we are not alone in this world. It is to be, in a real way, highly self-centered. Just as none of us can claim sole responsibility for our successes in life, none of us has been wounded or shaped only by our own actions. This is why the work of reflecting on our story, and being honest about it, matters.

Here's an example. Remember that couple from the beginning of the chapter, Alvah and Katie? Growing up my mother would often express her fear of "ending up in the poorhouse." My family was not just financially stable, but rather comfortable. We weren't rich, but no one was in any danger of "ending up in the poorhouse." In fact, there aren't poorhouses anymore. But my mother had inherited her family's fear of poverty, passed down by her grandmother and father. Even without knowing at a conscious level the specific story of her great-grandmother's divorce, poverty, and death, she knew that fear in a very real way and internalized it deeply, passing it on in turn to her own children.

One hundred years after the fact I wrestle with the same legacy. I pastor a church that gives me freedom in the pulpit and that has never tried to tell me what I can and cannot say in the pulpit. Even still, when I am about to preach a particularly difficult sermon, one with which people might not agree, the fears come back. What if the church gets angry? What if they fire me? What if I can't make ends meet? What if I end up . . . in the poorhouse?

24

In the end I had to learn to value the call to proclaim the truth, as I understood it, over the comfort and security of knowing I wouldn't ruffle any feathers. I had to trust the people I pastored and the fact that they were fair and open-minded, even when they didn't agree with me. I had to look at my fears, figure out where they came from, and resist the urge to let them call the shots.

To do this deeply personal internal work is, ironically, a step away from isolation. Dietrich Bonhoeffer writes in *The Cost of Discipleship* that "he who is alone with his sin is utterly alone."[12] That is true for all of us, whether the sin is our own or we are living with the effects of the sins of others. When we keep it locked inside, at least a part of us withdraws from community. Our fear of the truth alienates us from others and isolates us from the world. At best, we live without any kind of life-giving intimacy and, at worst, we move toward self-annihilation.

John Calvin writes at the beginning of *Institutes of the Christian Religion*, his major work, that knowledge of God and knowledge of self cannot be separated.[13] I think he's right. We cannot know ourselves until we know God. On the flip side, though, that also means that we cannot really know God if we do not know ourselves. If we lack the capacity to be self-reflective, we will never come to a place of true intimacy with God.

To choose another way is to choose life. To examine what we are holding on to in unhealthy ways, by whatever system or method feels right to us, is to choose to break the power of shame. It is not easy work to tell our own stories and to name the things that hold us back. To dare to break those chains, though, is an investment in our own freedom. As Jesus said, after all, the truth will indeed set us free.

THREE | RECONCILED

WHEN GOD RUNS TOWARD US

Jesus once told a story about a father who has two sons. One son is the dependable sort. He works on his dad's farm and does whatever he is told. The other? Not so much. This son comes to his father and asks to be given his share of the inheritance early. Taking it, he heads off to the big city, squanders it all, and ends up feeding pigs for a boss who feeds him even less.

One day the second son wakes up at rock bottom and remembers the loving father he has left behind. Maybe, he thinks to himself, I can see if there's room for me at my father's place. I know I can't be a son again, it's too late for that, but maybe he will let me work for him in the fields. With this hope, he leaves the city, daring to go back home.

Back on the farm the father is looking down the road. Scripture doesn't tell us that he was watching for the son he had lost, but I'd imagine he would look out into the distance sometimes, brokenheartedly waiting. So on the day when a figure appeared on the horizon, growing more familiar with every step, he knows in his heart who it is. Before the outline even becomes clear, he runs. He races down the road and through the dust, and he doesn't stop until his son is once again in his arms.

Our fear makes us run from God. We wind up in the belly of a whale instead of Nineveh. We find ourselves working for merciless masters instead of letting ourselves be loved. We run as resistance to mercy and grace, believing that, somehow, if we just run far enough, maybe we will be safe from our fear.

Sometimes, though, conversion happens. In faith circles when we use the word "conversion" we usually mean that someone has joined a new religion. I have always been a bit wary of the word, because I never want to be seen as someone who is trying to convert people to my faith, the way my fundamentalist classmates growing up in the South attempted to convert others.

I like the real idea of conversion, though. The Latin root word *convertere* literally means "to turn around." In chapter 1 we talked about recovery as running toward God. That's still true, but something funny starts happening the further you get in recovery. Eventually it becomes clear that all the while you've been running toward God, God's been running toward you. It took turning back around to see it.

Conversion is not a matter of coercion; it is something that happens between our hearts and God's. Conversion is the act of grace that lets us stop running away and starting turning around. Our conversion is not an act of religious initiation but a change of heart. It is turning toward the God who has been right behind us all along.

In the next part of our recovery journey our conversion continues. We stop running toward what cannot save us and in doing so stop running from the one who has always loved us. Contrary to what we have too often believed, in our turning around we discover that God does not want perfection . . . God just wants us.

WHOSE WE ARE

In chapter 2 we talked about learning to tell our stories truthfully. We examined how we became who we are, and we likely found that many people shaped us, for good or for ill. Our stories are bigger than us. None of us is self-made because it is impossible to disentangle ourselves from the ties that bind us to each other.

Our lives are shaped by our relationships. Our family of origin, our hometown, our friends, and our schools have all helped to define us. Our lives have also been shaped by what has happened to us. We cannot deny the power of the privileges and disadvantages that our various identities have bestowed on us. Finally, for those who have suffered pain or trauma for any reason, our exposure to those events impacts us long after they are over.

In short, our stories are bigger than us. Just as John Donne wrote that "no man is an island," our interdependence on one another cannot be overstated, nor can the harm that can come when that system of interdependence fails or hurts us. Understanding this is essential to telling the story of our lives and to understanding our identity.

For people of faith, though, we cannot tell our story without also telling the story of what God has done in our lives. To return to Bob Pazmino's idea, we must know who and whose we are; the two cannot be separated. In the end, regardless of what else has happened to us, our true identity is given to us not by the world, but by God.

In *Harry Potter and the Sorcerer's Stone*, the first book in the series, a traumatized boy who is approaching adolescence takes center stage. Orphaned, his suspicious and fearful extended family has kept him from learning the truth about himself. One day he receives a letter telling him that he has been accepted to a school called "Hogwarts." In that moment he learns not only that magic exists, but that he is a wizard. For the first time in his life, he has hope.

If only the same thing existed for children of God. There are no owls that fly parchment envelopes full of hope to us, avoiding the reach of the destructive voices in our lives. There's no letter that comes to us at age eleven saying "this is who you are, and it is good." Instead, we figure it out, a little at a time. If we are fortunate, we have people who help to guide us, but for far too many, we are left mostly on our own.

For those of us who would follow Christ, our primary identity comes not in our actions and not in what has happened to us, but in God's love for us. We have been "fearfully and wonderfully made," to quote Psalm 139, by a God who knows us at every level. "Where can I go from your spirit?" asks the psalmist. "Where can I flee from your presence? If I ascend to heaven, you are there; if I make my bed in Sheol, you are there." If there is nowhere we can go that is beyond God's presence, that means there is literally nowhere we can go that is beyond God's love and grace.

To put it another way, using the words of Romans 8:38–39, "For I am convinced that neither death, nor life, nor angels, nor rulers, nor things present, nor things to come, nor powers, nor height, nor depth, nor anything else in all creation, will be able to separate us from the love of God in Christ Jesus our Lord."

Recovery teaches us to find our identity in a power that is greater than ourselves. We are defined by the love and grace of a God who never leaves us. This is the same God who loves us at rock bottom, and the same God who runs after us when we run away. Just as we were not formed in isolation from the world, we are not formed in isolation from God. If we believe, or at least want to believe, that God is always with us, even if we don't feel it, that means that God's love and grace is always with us too. In the face of that truth, nothing in the world can exert greater defining power over us. We are already claimed; this is our true identity.

In the first two chapters we have begun our conversion. We have stopped running away and started turning back to a God who has been with us all along. In this chapter we will examine our estrangement from God. Here we examine the spiritual barriers that are blocking our way out of the tomb, and we begin to remove them.

It is important to acknowledge that this is lifelong work and that for some of us this comes easier than for others. That is especially true if you have been wounded by the church or by Christians in any way. It takes real courage to claim your spiritual journey back and to clear your path of the spiritual debris that has been placed by others. The fact that you might dare to open yourself again is evidence that God's grace is bigger that anything a toxic faith community might do.

In recovery communities we often use the phrase "came to believe" to describe our spiritual journeys. Few of us came in the door without being in some way estranged from God. The return of our faith, and of conscious connection with God, did not happen in one fell swoop. It was a slow process of strengthening and conversion, in the literal sense of that word. We learned to turn away from what could never love us and turn toward the only one who always has. This is how we learned to live again.

RECONCILIATION

Much of the work of recovery is the work of reconciliation. We learn to be in right relationship with God, self, and neighbor. We move deliberately from the work of identity to intimacy, not in a linear fashion as Erikson suggests, but in a circular one, understanding more about ourselves as we better engage God and God's creation. We begin this reconciliatory work by looking at our own relationship with God.

First, though, what does reconciliation even mean? To really understand it we return, again, to the root of a word. The Latin word *concilare*, meaning "to make friendly," forms the base, with the prefix "*re-*" meaning "again." To reconcile is to literally "make friendly again." So reconciliation can only happen, and only needs to happen, when a relationship is broken.

In the previous chapter we told the truth about our brokenness. We have been shattered by our own actions and those of others. In our relationship with God, we have been separated by this brokenness. At its most basic level, sin is simply separation from God. What that definition doesn't make clear, though, is that the sins causing that separation are not always our own. Sometimes systemic sin, which perpetuates injustice in the world, and sometimes the sins of those who have or had power over us create barriers between our hearts and God. And, yes, sometimes our own personal brokenness and sin creates that barrier too.

Many Christians believe that our salvation, whatever that looks like for us, is guaranteed by Jesus's crucifixion on Good Friday. For them, a literal blood atonement has to take place in which God makes Christ bear the punishment for our sin. I have always wrestled with that, because I don't believe a God of grace, a loving spiritual parent, could ever kill their child out of a need for the "justice" of punishment.

To me, Jesus's crucifixion was one more sign of the brokenness of the world. A good man who did God's will constantly, and who offered the world hope, was seen as such a great threat by those in power that they killed him. I don't believe Jesus's death was necessary for us to be reconciled to God, but I do believe it points to another reason why that reconciliation needs to happen.

Instead, I believe that our salvation takes place in incarnation and resurrection. Incarnation is just the fancy theological way of saying "God becomes one of us." Christians generally believe that Jesus was God incarnate, or God in human form in the person of Jesus Christ. Around Advent, when we sing "O Come, O Come, Emmanuel" we are calling out for Jesus, who is Emmanuel, literally "God with us" to be born.

To use the story from the prologue, in the incarnation God chooses to "get in the hole" with us. God comes into a broken world and participates in its transformation. God doesn't stand at the edge, looking down at us saying, "I wish you the best getting back up." God, like the good friend, jumps in and begins the process of reconciliation.

Likewise, in resurrection Jesus shows us that there is a way out of the tombs, out of the hole, and into new life. After resurrection, though, God does not stay on the safe edges up above, looking down at us. If we believe that God is everywhere and that nothing can separate us from the love and grace God, that means God is down with us at the bottom of the hole, ready to guide us out.

For those of us who have ever found ourselves at the bottom looking up, this is an invitation. How do we respond to God's presence with us? Do we choose to stay in, believing new life is impossible? Or do we accept God's invitation to us to climb out? God loves us at our various rock bottoms in life, but God does not force us to accept help. Grace helps us turn to God, but our response to that grace, irresistible as it may be, at some level has to be our own.

Reconciliation must be a voluntary process. The reconciliation God offers to us, a repaired relationship that brings healing, is beautiful, but it not easy. God's love and grace will be with us even if we say "no" to it, but the fullness of the life we can have will not come until we respond. Grace can bring us to our knees and show us that something is wrong, but until we truly want to get well and to heal our brokenness, we will remain in the tombs.

In recovery we choose, sometimes tentatively, to respond to God's offer of new life. We let God love us out of the places of death and into the places of resurrection. We become friendly again, not just with God, but with ourselves and with the world. If we do this well, we even become people of gratitude instead of people of fear.

SAFE THUS FAR

Take a minute and think back to your story. Retell it in your mind, or even put it down on paper. At this point your comfort level with it might vary. Most of our stories offer both joy and heartbreak. Anger, pain, and regret may feel close at hand right now. For some of us, the wounds of our past never quite healed correctly. Recovery makes us reopen scars, and reset badly mended bones. There's nothing easy about that, and no quick fix. You might be feeling worse now than you did before.

I sure did in early recovery. Not only did I have to look at hard truths, but I had to do it without the help of my addiction, the thing that made the pain and regret go away. In my first year or two there were times when I wondered whether I was better off sober. Had things really been that bad?

Relapse is common in early recovery, and I think a big reason for that is we have to start grappling with the truth. The addictions and unhealthy behaviors from which we seek to recover will do all they can to trick us into believing we are fine. The best way to defeat this self-sabotage, though, is to identity the false promises of whatever is holding us back from full life, because nothing in our history is so terrible that God cannot overcome it.

There is a line in "The Promises," a section of the Big Book, that proclaims that if we do this work faithfully, "we will not regret the past nor wish to shut the door on it."[14] That seemed unbelievable to me as a newcomer. I had so many regrets and had wasted so much time. How could I ever stop beating myself up for that?

What helped was learning to look at my story in a new way. I began to look at my past as a spiritual journey. I took comfort in St. Augustine's Confessions and other spiritual autobiographies that didn't sugarcoat the truth. St. Augustine was one of the greatest saints of the church, and even he had led a reckless youth. Who was I to believe that my past was so shameful, that God could not use me?

I began to tell my story again, this time looking for the ways that God had been a part of it. What I had previously seen as wasted years were now times of learning and transformation. I was able to look at the places where God interceded and gave me just enough grace to steer clear of disaster. I could find evidence of God's love even in the lowest places. Now I also saw clearly the places where I had run, and now I could name the places where fear and false idols had stood in the way of God.

In telling our story again at this stage we move from the question "How did I become me?" to "Where was God in that process?" Even in the hardest moments, we often find that we can see evidence of God's presence in retrospect. This is not about dismissing past pain with a platitude about God not "giving us more than we can handle." This is about telling the truth about the ways we have been broken and seeing that, even in the aftermath of the greatest pain, the kind that God never wills upon us, God is still there. In fact, while God does not will bad things to happen to us, God can use those of us who have survived them in order to transform the world.

In this retelling we also learn that we are more than just our history. We must be, because God is in it, and if our story is big enough for God, then it must be a story not just for the past and for the present, but for the future. Our lives to date have prepared us for the story that we will keep writing. The only difference is that now we will write that story with the knowledge that God is with us on every page. We are transformed from documenters of pain and regret into artists of hope and possibility.

In his book *The Return of the Prodigal Son*, Henri Nouwen writes, "People who have come to know the joy of God do not deny the darkness, but they choose not to live in it."[15] The Serenity Prayer teaches us that we cannot change everything, but that we can ask for courage to choose to change the things we can. We often have more agency than we know. Oppressive systems and life experiences too often make us believe otherwise. To come to understand this, and to come to know that God is standing with us in the face of what robs us of life, is to realize that we have power we never imagined.

MAKING AMENDS

Before we can claim this power, though, comes responsibility. One of the primary tools the twelve steps uses is the making of amends. This process is typically understood as an interpersonal one, between you and those you may have hurt in the past. While that work is indeed important, it is also work that any relationship of intimacy must undertake. This includes our relationship with God, and our relationship with ourselves.

Steps five through seven of the twelve steps focus on being honest with God and asking for help. They read:

5. Admitted to God, to ourselves, and to another human being the exact nature of our wrongs.

6. Were entirely ready to have God remove all these defects of character.

7. Humbly asked [God] to remove our shortcomings.

In step five we move out of our shame, and we get honest with God. The good news is that we are not telling God anything that God doesn't already know. God already knows, and God loves us still. As in any healthy relationship, though, we have to be able to tell the one we love the truth. If we really want reconciliation, and an honest relationship, we can't hold any part of ourselves back when we come to God.

Steps five through seven are similar to corporate prayers of confession in church on Sunday. We are simply saying that we are not perfect and that we need help. When we pray the prayer of confession we tell God that we are ready to live differently, and we ask God to help us see that change through. That is the work of steps six and seven: being ready to try a new way and asking God to help us.

In these steps we are accomplishing two things. First, we are showing God that we know the places we have gone off course, and we are telling God that we are sorry for that. Like any real apology, though, we are also committing to change. We have had enough of saying we are sorry and then going back out and doing the same thing again and again. This time we are asking God to help us.

In making these amends to God, we also begin to let go of shame. We all carry shame with us in some way. It's healthy to know when we have gone off course, necessary even, but it's not healthy to live in shame because of it. Shame is corrosive, and it undermines the good gifts that God has given us to use in the world. Sometimes we become so buried in our own shame that we become immobilized by it, believing ourselves to be so far beyond redemption that we can do nothing right.

I truly believe that God does not want us to live in shame. God wants us to be honest and to turn away from what is destroying us, but God doesn't want us to hate ourselves or believe we are useless. God wouldn't have jumped into the hole for us if we were worthless. The father would not have run to the prodigal son and celebrated his return, either. When the son returned home, the father did not shame him or send him out to work off his sin. Instead, he threw a party and told everyone his son was back.

Letting go of our shame frees us to know the fullness of God's love. It also reconciles us to God by freeing us to do God's will in the world. God can use us in new ways because what we have survived can allow us to more authentically serve others who face the same struggles. Shame obscures the image of God that is in us all, but reconciliation with God strips that shame away.

There is a verse in the well-known hymn "Amazing Grace": "Through many dangers, toils, and snares / I have already come. / 'Tis grace has brought me safe thus far / And grace will lead me home." That verse symbolizes so much of what it means to be reconciled with God. We look back at our lives, and we find the places where God's grace has carried us through. We turn back to God, and we say that we want to do things differently. We tell the truth, and we find that we are loved and full of worth. We leave rock bottom, and we let grace lead us back to a home where one who loves us runs to hold us once again. This is our reconciliation with God, and this is the foundation of our hope.

F O U R | W H O L E

MARTIN LUTHER AND THE MONASTERY

Before Martin Luther was the father of the Protestant Reformation, he was an anxious young man. Luther was worried that God did not love him and that he would be damned to hell for the most trivial of his sins. Faith was not a comfort to him, but a source of constant fear.

One day, when he was about twenty-one years old and beginning his law studies, Luther was caught outside in a terrible thunderstorm. Lighting struck so close to him that he was thrown to the ground, believing he was about to die. Terrified, he called out to God, promising to become a monk if God would only let him survive.

Luther made good on his promise and entered the monastery. Far from settling into unquestioning obedience, though, this was where Luther wrestled with his biggest spiritual questions. Luther struggled to reconcile what he was learning about the Bible with the church that he knew. As he read the letter to the Romans he became convinced that we are saved by grace, and not by our own good works.

His view of God changed. Luther began to believe that maybe God really did love him, that maybe the church he had known all his life was the one who was wrong.

With this new understanding of God, Luther realized that his life must change, and so he did the unimaginable: he left the monastery. Dietrich Bonhoeffer, the theologian and martyr who died at the hands of the Nazis, writes about this part of Luther's life: "The bottom having thus been knocked out of the religious life, Luther laid hold upon grace. Just as the whole world of monasticism was crashing about him in ruins he saw God in Christ stretching forth his hand to save . . . [and that grace] shattered his whole existence."[16]

Grace is tricky that way. When we really come to understand that God loves us, and that we are created "good," it would seem that life would get easier. But, as Luther and later Bonhoeffer both knew well, grace is not "cheap."[17] Far from allowing us to keep living life the way we always have, grace troubles our mind and spirit until we cannot help but respond. Martin Luther, safe in the knowledge that he was loved and saved by God, could have sat back and enjoyed his life in the monastery, reading and teaching. Grace, however, wouldn't allow that. That's because grace forces us out of our safe places and into the world; grace makes us change—and gives us the courage to change.

RECONCILING WITH OURSELVES

We will return to Luther, but first let's look at the big picture of recovery. In chapter 2 we thought about our own story and how we came to be who we are now. In chapter 3 we reexamined that story and asked where God was present. In this chapter we come back to our stories again, aware of the grace of God in our lives, and ask, "What's next?"

In this chapter we are standing between two great loves and working on the third. The last chapter was about the love of God, and the next is about the love of neighbor. This chapter is about learning to love ourselves, in all our fullness. There is a deliberateness to this order. When Jesus was asked what the greatest commandment was he responded, "You shall love the Lord your God with all your heart, and with all your soul, and with all your mind. This is the greatest and first commandment. And a second is like it, you shall love your neighbor as yourself" (Matt. 22:36–38).

These are the three great loves that Christ calls us to, and their order matters. In learning to love God, we learn how much God loves us. We are created by a God who does not abandon us. God loves us enough to become one of us, to jump down in the hole with us and show us a way out. In that act we learn that we are beloved, that God has claimed us as God's own, and that God has cast God's lot in with us. This is amazing, and it is beautiful. It is also, as Luther well knew, highly inconvenient.

Learning that we are loved by God means that we have to acknowledge that maybe we are worth loving. It's hard to stress how countercultural an idea this is, even (maybe especially) in the twenty-first century. Entire churches, industries, political movements, and more are devoted to telling us that we should not love ourselves, that we are not good enough, and that until we change we are worthless. God cuts through that nonsense and tells you that you are loved. Period. There's nothing you can do about it. How can we argue with that?

To know that God loves you is to know that you must love yourself. Your very identity comes from the fact that you are God's beloved. You are worth more than what you tell yourself on your worst days. God knows every bit of your history, every thing that you have kept hidden from others and even yourself, and God still loves you wildly. God has been with you every step of the journey, just waiting for you to turn around and remember who you are.

There's a story in the book of Genesis about Jacob coming across a man who begins wrestling with him. All night they grapple until the man tells Jacob to let him go. Jacob refuses, saying, "I will not let you go until you bless me." It is only when Jacob is blessed that he learns he has been wrestling with God all night, has seen God face-to-face, and has lived to tell about it. In the morning light, God renames Jacob "Israel," or "wrestles with God" (Gen. 32:22–31).

For some of us, our journey to this point has felt less like a walk with God and more like a wrestling match. We have fought with ourselves, and we have grappled with God. We have refused to let go, desperate for some sign of a blessing. It has not been easy, but even at the end of the longest night, God has still been there in the morning, ready to bless us. In fact, our blessing, like Jacob's, comes in large part from the fact that we dared to grapple with God and not let go.

If we can wrestle with God and receive a blessing, what happens when we wrestle with the very real work of loving ourselves? If God can bless us, why are we so reluctant to bless and love ourselves? What would it look like if we stopped fighting ourselves and started to accept that, if God loves us enough to stay connected, maybe we should start loving ourselves too?

In recovery we have a saying: "To thine own self be true." It's actually borrowed from *Hamlet*, but it works well for people who are trying to live transformed lives. When we say it we are reminding ourselves to never do what feels at odds with who we know ourselves to be. It's about respecting ourselves enough to not indulge in the things that want to kill us. For those of us who follow Christ, though, it could mean this: Your true self is the you who belongs to God and is loved by God, so don't treat yourself as anything less than God's beloved.

Until we can learn to be true to, and love, ourselves, we cannot fulfill the second part of the great commandment. How can we "love our neighbors as ourselves" if we do not know how to love ourselves? If all we know how to do is treat ourselves terribly, we will never do better when it comes to others. We cannot hope to do effective work with others, even with our closest friends, until we know and love ourselves.

I'm reminded of when a couple comes to me for premarital counseling, intent on getting married immediately. It sometimes becomes clear that neither party has ever really figured out who they are, and yet here they are about to make a lifelong commitment to someone else. The odds of the marriage lasting and being healthy are not good. The partners are trying to find their identity, rather than intimacy, in one another. When I do premarital counseling with partners who have done their own work ahead of time, though, people who have wrestled with God and themselves, I know the marriage will likely be a long and happy one.

William Sloane Coffin put it this way: "Just as a stream has no chance of running deep until it finds its banks, so we, until we have discovered our limits, haven't a prayer of becoming profound."[18] If we don't know who we are and where our own boundaries lie, we will be perpetually shallow, useless to our neighbors and the world. Until we dare to reconcile with ourselves, we risk being spread so thin that we will run dry. If, however, we dare to do the work of knowing and loving ourselves, we become deep and strong. We become people of character and courage.

LOVING YOURSELF, EVEN WHEN THE WORLD DOESN'T

I know that at least some of the world wants me dead. That might sound stark, but it's true. I'm female-bodied, gay, gender nonconforming, in a same-sex marriage, more than a little stocky, and the sort of person who doesn't easily shut up when I feel like something unjust is happening. This is deeply inconvenient to some, and outright infuriating to others.

The reactions of others used to bother me. I spent my youth and early young adult years trying to take up as little space as possible. I wanted to change, but not in ways that were true to myself. If I just dressed a little less masculine, I'd reason, things would be fine. Or if I swallowed my words and stood back when I saw injustice happening, then I could rise to a position where I could actually do something about it. If I succeeded, on others' terms, then maybe I could love myself.

I tried to love myself right out of existence. That happens far too often. The world wants some part of us dead, and we too often oblige. It's the reason addictions, compulsions, and eating disorders are in no short supply. When everything around you tells you that you are wrong, you start to believe it. Shame becomes the constant shackle that holds you back, and you start to hate yourself enough to destroy yourself.

Recovery taught me that loving myself wasn't just a nice thing to try to do; it was a radical act. To love ourselves in a world that literally profits off of our self-hatred is an act of resistance. The poet e. e. cummings wrote, "To be nobody-but-yourself—in a world which is doing its best, night and day, to make you everybody else—means to fight the hardest battle which any human being can fight; and never stop fighting."[19] To wrestle daily with the world, and to dare to live as the person who God has created you to be, is to embody resistance.

In the last chapter we talked about making amends to God, and finding reconciliation. The other side of that process is making amends to ourselves. Think of all the times in your life when you have hated yourself, or harmed yourself in any way, because you did not measure up to what you thought you should be. What joy have you not allowed yourself to feel out of a belief that you didn't deserve it? What opportunities have you turned down for fear of being an imposter? What parts of yourself have you loved, but then destroyed in order to be loved by others?

You already carry the consequences inside of yourself for these things. Don't beat yourself up again, because you've been hard at work doing that already, consciously or unconsciously. Instead, acknowledge them. Tell yourself that you love yourself too much to let it happen again. And then let it go. Don't use this as another reason to hate yourself. Use it as an opportunity to love yourself the way that God loves you; come back home from your exile, and find a celebration upon your return.

Forgiving ourselves goes against everything that this world tells us to do. That's all the more reason to do it. When we accept God's desire to reconcile with us, and when we reconcile with ourselves, we are creating hope. We are also becoming people who can reconcile with others and help the world to reconcile with itself. People who cannot do this work within themselves will be unable to do it with the world. In fact, those who cannot love themselves are likely to be deeply destructive to others. But for those who can do this work? The possibilities are beyond our imagination.

INTEGRITY OR FRAGMENTATION?

When I was twenty-one, I entered seminary. I was a candidate for ministry in the Presbyterian Church (USA). At the time, the Presbyterian Church stated that same-sex relationships were a barrier for ordination. Officially, if you were gay you couldn't be a minister. This was a challenge for me because I already knew I was gay. I had been out for about four years at this point. Even still, taking the advice of many older mentors and advisors, I did what most other gay candidates at the time did and participated in the "don't ask, don't tell" culture of ordination. I said that if my ordination committee ever asked me directly whether I was gay, I would not lie. They never did, and so three years later I was ordained. What I didn't understand at the time, though, was how deeply my soul was suffering.

The reconciled person is the integrated person. When we are torn between who we truly are and who we believe we should be, we become fragmented. Our hearts are divided between two different sets of values and behaviors, and we lose our way. Conversely, when our values, actions, and realities align, and when we know our true identity, we become powerfully integrated.

Most of us try to be people of integrity. The words integrity and integrated come from the same Latin root word, which means "whole." People of integrity literally seek to be whole and try to align their actions with their values. The person they present in public is the same as the one in private, and their words match their true beliefs and feelings. People of integrity know their values because they know who and whose they are, and they refuse to forget it.

The love of God and our love of ourselves help us to become people of integrity. When we know that God's love has claimed us and we learn to love ourselves truly, it becomes harder to do anything that denigrates that love. Our reconciliation with God and ourselves becomes a true act of integration, pulling the pieces of us that have been kept apart back together. To use Erik Erikson's language, the integrated, or reconciled, self has both a strong sense of identity, as well as a sense of intimacy with God and with self. Love is what has put us back together.

This would not be a surprise to Martin Luther. Just as Jacob wrestled all night with God, Luther wrestled with God's grace in the monastery. Once he knew for certain who and whose he was, he could not stay. To be an integrated person, to be a person of integrity, he had to leave the monastery and speak his truth, no matter the cost.

I believe everyone has a struggle like Luther's, though ours may be a bit less dramatic. When I got sober, for instance, five years after my Presbyterian ordination, I began to examine why my drinking had escalated. I realized that, for me, the "don't ask, don't tell" mandate of my denomination was harmful. Having to skirt around the subject while in ministry settings was exhausting. I was living every day in shame. There was the shame of hiding the truth about myself from a church I loved dearly, and the shame of not being proud of who God made me to be. Though I told myself that I knew who I was, and that one day things would change in my church, I was living a fragmented life.

I still deeply love the Presbyterian Church, but one of my first major decisions after my first year of sobriety was to begin the process of transferring my ordination to a denomination where I would not need to hide. I had responded to the fragmentation of self in a way that now makes a lot of sense. Just as Jesus taught, I could not serve two masters. I could not be who I was and also be who the church demanded I be. I had become self-destructive. In order to live a sober life, I had to remove all the barriers to integration that I could. Leaving my church was a step on the road to integrity.

After leaving the Presbyterian Church I felt a deep sense of inner peace, or what we in recovery call serenity. I was finally living with deep integrity. This is not to say that things were perfect or that I did not mourn having to leave my church. It is to say that at the end of each day I could look at myself in the mirror knowing that I was exactly who I said that I was, and exactly who God made me to be. One of the greatest lessons that recovery has taught me is that serenity can never truly be present without integrity.

RIGHT-SIZED

Recovery has taught me another lesson about integrity, which is that a truly integrated person is also a right-sized person. "Right-sized" is another recovery concept that translates well to the wider world. We strive to be "right-sized" by being "not too big" and "not too small" in our opinions of ourselves. Being right-sized means respecting and valuing yourself, but also keeping your ego in check.

It may sound odd to talk about humility in a chapter about learning to love one's self, but the two go hand in hand. In her book *Quiet: The Power of Introverts in a World That Can't Stop Talking*, Susan Cain argues that we have ceased to be a Culture of Character and have instead become a Culture of Personality. Drawing on the theories of

Warren Susman, Cain writes that in the time of Character, "What counted was not so much the impression one made in public as how one behaved in private." In the time of Personality, however, "Americans started to focus on how others perceived them. They became captivated by people who were bold and entertaining."[20]

We live in an age where reality show stars can dominate serious news sources and even be elevated to high political office. We have become a culture that rewards narcissism and shuns humility. Even once-subdued spiritual writers have jumped onboard, rushing to sell memoirs of their latest turmoil before they've even had time to process it themselves. Everything is for the consumption of others, and not for the transformation of the interior life. Personality sells. Character? Not so much.

Humility is an antidote to the Culture of Personality, especially if it is properly understood. We are apt to hear the word "humility" today and equate it with "humiliation," which is absolutely not what I'm talking about here. Humility, in its truest sense, is really just being right-sized. It means understanding that you are no better than others, but it also means refusing to allow yourself to be denigrated.

Paul Tillich, the twentieth-century theologian, once argued that the main reason for sin was human pride. Feminist theologians read his work and took exception. They argued that for women, and for those who have faced other kinds of oppression, a lack of pride was just as deadly. The work of the Christian is to come to understand and love themselves as God's beloved, and to also understand and love others as God's beloved as well. While we are all different and possess different strengths and gifts worthy of use and appreciation, we are not inherently more special than anyone else. Nor are we any less special. To understand that is to be right-sized.

This is a crucial distinction to make at this stage of recovery because so many of us are not right-sized when we begin this work. We believe we are worthless, underserving of God's love or our own. Or we think that we are exceedingly special, and that only the other truly gifted of this world can really love or understand us. Perhaps most perplexing, many of us manage to be both at the same time, spending half our time hating ourselves and half our time thinking we are superior. In recovery we call that being "an egomaniac with an inferiority complex." It's more common than we may think.

True humility teaches us another way. It helps us to navigate a diverse world with integrity, bringing our best selves to every interaction while being open to the wisdom that we might receive from others. Humility is the ultimate corrective to narcissism which, far from a simple overabundance of self love, is really about an inability to truly receive love. Narcissism is like an open void that can never be filled, a deep longing for love and admiration that will never be satisfied. Narcissism is the sign of a self that is so fragmented that humility is impossible.

We all struggle with wanting to be special. We all also wrestle with the fear that we are not. The gift of recovery is that these fears begin to fade into the background. Instead of letting them define our lives, we choose to be defined by God's love for us and our love for ourselves. We find a place of integration and peace. We become more able to engage with our friends and communities, and later the world at large. When we do these things as right-sized people, full of integrity, we are already leading lives of resistance. We refuse to be what the world tells us that we must be. We choose a better way for ourselves, and we make a better way for others.

AMENDS

Part of being right-sized is learning to be in right relationship with others. One of the scariest parts of the twelve steps for newcomers is the idea of making amends, or saying "I'm sorry" to others. Forgiveness can be a terrifying thing for anyone to ask for, but making amends with others is a critical part of the healing process.

In step eight we are asked to have made "a list of persons we had harmed, and became willing to make amends to them all" and in step nine to have made "direct amends to such people wherever possible, except when to do so would injure them or others." Amends are for the people we have hurt, because they deserve an apology, but there's a personal aspect to this as well. In saying that we are sorry, by owning up to what we have done, we are also saying that we are willing to face the truth and to move on.

When we can admit that we have been wrong, and apologize, we will find that we are no longer defined by the worst things we have done. Regardless of whether or not we find forgiveness, we are at least given the freedom to start rebuilding on a clean foundation. We might find a reconciliation that we never expected, or we might not. In either case, we are given the chance to let go and to define ourselves by our future, not our past mistakes.

As we move further into recovery, integrity and humility will guide us well. They will also help us as we continue to write the story of our lives. Up to this point we have written a story that answered some big questions: How did I become me? Where was God? What does it look like for me to be whole? We have learned that we have been formed by what has happened to us, but we have also learned that our story is bigger than that too.

We are becoming integrated people, able to see our story and God's at the same time, and to start loving ourselves back to wholeness. Now we are moving into the next piece of reconciliation work by learning what it means to be in positive community with others. Here our identity work starts to more fully become intimacy work as we seek to love our neighbor and allow them to love us. We find the friends, allies, and communities that will walk with us along the way. We also learn an essential lesson of resistance: none of us can do this alone.

St. Francis de Sales once said, "Be who you are, and be that well." My hope is that you are learning more each day about who you truly are, and whose. You are God's beloved, created for amazing things. You are about to reengage with a world of others who are just the same. Imagine the possibilities if we all met one another being exactly who we are, and being that well.

F I V E | C O N N E C T E D

SEARCHING FOR LIFE IN DEAD WATER

When I was a pastor in Vermont I took up fly fishing. I had always
wanted to learn, and I was living in the backyard of the Green Mountain National Forest, where legendary trout streams emerge. I figured
that I would buy a fly rod and reel and be landing trout in no time,
just like a scene right out of *A River Runs Through It*.

It didn't happen that way. Instead I spent afternoons driving out
on unpaved forest roads, looking for signs of water on topographic
maps. I would hike back to picturesque mountain lakes, choose the
exact fly my hatch guide recommended, and cast carefully into the
water. And then . . . nothing.

Finally I sheepishly went to the well-known fly-fishing outfitters
a few towns over, found the best fishing guide I knew, and asked,
"What am I doing wrong?" The guide was patient with me and lis-
tened to my descriptions of every place I'd cast a line. Then he nodded
and delivered his diagnosis: "You're fishing in dead water."

I'd heard of "living water" before, but "dead water" wasn't a term I knew. It turns out that dead water, at least as this guide used it, is a body of water where fish cannot thrive. Because of human-made pollution, a lack of oxygen or circulation, changing water temperatures, or a number of other factors, the water becomes hostile to life. The fish begin to die, and the ecological landscape is transformed for the worst.

Literal water has a lot to teach us about "living water." Jesus uses the metaphor of "living water" when he meets the Samaritan woman at the well. Jesus crosses a social barrier and asks her for a drink. Stunned that a man, and a non-Samaritan one at that, would ask her for anything, she asks Jesus what he's thinking. "Why do you, a Jewish man, ask for something to drink from me, a Samaritan woman?" Jesus flips the question, saying that if she knew who he was, she'd be asking him for "living water," the kind that "will become in those who drink it a spring of water that bubbles up into eternal life" (John 4:9, 13–14 CEB).

What Jesus is offering to the woman, and to the world, is renewal. Living water is a metaphor for spiritual vitality. Just as water is life, and it is not offered in isolation, Jesus dares to cross the lines that have been drawn and to risk intimacy with another. By his very example, Jesus tells us that we cannot have full life without connections beyond ourselves.

Dead waters are often isolated from streams and other sources of new water. Unmoved by incoming tides, they become stagnant. Isolation can kill entire bodies of water. How much more true is that for us? We are at least 50 percent water, after all. We are more than the things that make up our bodies, but maybe there's something to that?

Erikson understood this when he wrote about the importance of intimacy. After identity, it is our last major hurdle before we can lead generative, impactful lives. Our intimacy with God matters, as does our intimacy with ourselves. Just as Jesus told us in his greatest commandment, though, they are incomplete if we do not also have intimacy with our neighbors. To love our neighbor as ourselves, we must dare to cross the lines from isolation to connection.

In the baptismal vows of most Christian traditions, the one being baptized (or their parents) promises to remain connected to the gathered community of Christ. There is no such thing as a Lone Ranger Christian. We need one another. We rely on the nurture, guidance, support, and teaching of our communities. There is a reason that Jesus called the church his own body. If that is true, that means the church too is part of the living waters. That also means that to isolate oneself from the community of faith is to risk drifting into dead waters.

The same is true of anyone who works for justice and against oppression. In any struggle for good, we need community. We draw our strength from one another, and we help one another to stay the course. If we are at our best, we work together to make the waters where we live a safe and healthy place for all. We also learn to recognize when we are in dead or toxic waters, and what our responsibility is when we find ourselves in those places. Taken together, this is the work of reconciliation and healthy connection crucial for making this world habitable for all.

LIFE-GIVING CONNECTIONS

On that first day of sobriety I sat in my car ready to give just about anything to not have to go inside the building. When I finally worked up the courage to go inside, I crept into the back of a meeting. Over and over people spoke, giving their names and the classic qualifier: "and I'm an alcoholic." I was uncomfortable enough sitting in back, but at least I didn't have to say anything.

But then the end of the meeting came, and a man stood up and started giving out colored-coded coins signifying how long someone had stayed sober. "Nine months?" he asked. "Six?" "Three?" "Thirty days?" I marveled at the people standing up, taking the metal coins as others clapped. How did they make it a month? Or three? Or more? And that's when the final chip came. Small and silver, the man up front asked if anyone in the room was there who wanted to give sobriety a try. I tried to hide my fleeting, uncomfortable glance, but he caught my eye and held out a coin, cocking his head to the side and saying, "It binds us to you; not you to us."

I guess those were the words I needed to hear. I wasn't so sure I was ready for this journey they were inviting me to take, but these people I had never met before were offering to support me. They had all been down this same road before, and they were willing to walk it with me. Put another way, I was down at the bottom of a hole, and they were ready to jump on in, no questions asked.

Our communities often become a kind of living water for us. When we are in danger of isolation and stagnation, they rush in and revive us. The recovery community taught me how important it is to do that for one another. In fact, when some newcomers to sobriety struggle with the concept of having God as a "Higher Power" they are encouraged to just think about the greater fellowship, all the others who have gone through what they are going through now, as their Higher Power instead. That's not to say that the group wishes to take the place of God; they simply want to help the person feel like they have somewhere to turn while they answer the larger questions for themselves.

It is this sense of belonging that is crucial for those who wish to grow. We need communities that will love us in our struggles. In many ways the recovery community taught me more about church than church. In recovery communities every person present knows grace. They know what it means to hit rock bottom and to find a way out. Even if it's your first time there, you know at some level that there's another way.

When communities are at their best, we all benefit. To go back to Erik Erikson's work, communities teach us how to have intimacy with others, and they validate our identity. A good church, just like any other good community, will teach us more about "who and whose" we are and will help us to find others on the same journey. Eventually our understanding of "whose" we are will even expand to include the communities that give us life.

Recall the Harry Potter example from a previous chapter, when Harry first received his Hogwart's letter: that was when he learned who he was—a wizard. It was not until Harry went to Hogwarts, though, that he learned what that meant. It took having community to understand where he belonged or what his life could be. In the end, it was only because he had community that he was able to resist the greatest threat to his life and to his friends' lives. Good communities love us, teach us, and form us. They make us more ourselves, in a way. They take the identity we bring, and make it deeper and richer. They refuse to let us stagnate or isolate.

TOXIC WATERS

It would be naive to think, though, that every community is a healthy one. Just as some communities can show us what living water looks like, others can show us what toxic water means. Just as the pollution and lack of light killed off trout in some of the Vermont streams where I tried to fish, there is a great deal of harm that can be done when we don't take care of our communities.

The theologian Karl Barth was once asked in a lecture to define what "church" means. This was a man who had written volume upon volume of complex systematic theology books, so his answer took some of those in attendance by surprise. "Church," he said simply, "is wherever two or more are gathered, and you are known at your deepest level." In other words, church is where you can be all of yourself, and where you find that others recognize you and know that you belong there too. This is why it is so important to find a community where you are free to be who you are, and who God made you to be.

What makes good churches vital is the same thing that makes recovery groups grow year after year. Going to a place where people can come and be completely honest, and then be met with nothing but belonging and love, is like falling into a river of living water. The community where we can bring all of who we are is the only kind that is truly living, and it is the only kind that truly deserves us. On the other hand, the community that tells you that you must be anything less than your full and true self will only stagnate, and it will take you down with it.

Church communities are not unique in their corruptibility. Every organization, no matter how well intentioned, can be transformed from full-of-life to toxic. When it happens in faith communities, though, it is especially unsettling. We would like to think that we are better than this, or somehow immune to it. We are not. Admitting that is crucial to ensuring that it does not happen on our watch.

In 2014, then Episcopal Bishop Heather Cook killed bicyclist Thomas Palermo while driving drunk. In the aftermath of the crash, she fled the scene before returning and being arrested. A breathalyzer showed that her blood-alcohol content was three times the legal limit. Soon after, news broke that this was Cook's second arrest for driving under the influence.

Parishioners learned that the diocese had been aware of Cook's previous arrest but had decided not to have her disclose it during her election. Later it was revealed that Cook had been heavily drinking at a preconsecration dinner, making it clear to the other bishops present that she was not sober and did not have her alcohol use under control. Despite the concerns, the consecration went forward.[21]

I certainly believe that recovering alcoholics can serve effectively as clergy. That's different from a clergy person who is clearly in the midst of an addiction crisis and who does not seem to taking the necessary steps to seek recovery. That person should not be actively serving in any ministry, let alone be elevated to bishop. Why in the world had her diocese, and the wider church, not intervened?

While I am not privy to the inside conversations, I have seen something similar happen enough to know the likely answer: church people are great enablers. Christians have an addiction to being nice. We do not want to disturb the peace, cause anyone discomfort, or risk conflict. Instead, we let things slide, reasoning that we are all imperfect, and hoping everything will work out for the best.

That may be the way to make sure that you have a conflict-free community (at least for a little while) but that's the exact opposite of having a healthy community. Enablers, in the parlance of addiction, are the people who make it possible for an addict to continue their behavior. They look the other way, make excuses, diminish consequences, and otherwise protect the addict and the institution. In reality they are helping to destroy both and failing to protect others.

Almost every congregation and denomination has some sort of history of people in power behaving in dangerous ways while others enable them. It might be a leader with an addiction, or it might be a clergy person who uses their position to abuse those in their care. It could be a refusal to ask why the financial records never quite add up, or it might be a reluctance to ask why the youth leader's wife has a black eye. It might be that committee member who bullies every new pastor who comes through the door, or the member who makes inappropriate jokes to the women at coffee hour. Whatever it is, when we become enablers our communities suffer.

A friend of mine who worked in a ministry setting where decades of abuse were uncovered told me once about a new series of revelations, and the wonder at how this had been covered up for so long. Looking at me in exasperation my friend said flatly, "This whole place needs Al-Anon."[22] To be sure, this was a place filled with good people who wanted to do the right thing, but they had never learned how to stop enabling bad behavior by hiding it.

Too many churches confuse confidentiality with secrecy. We have a mandate to hold some things in confidence, such as what a pastor hears during a pastoral counseling session. We do not have a mandate to keep secrets. Secrets in churches are almost always corrosive. Just as the saying "we are as sick as our secrets" implies, our communal secrets also eat away at us, both as individuals and communities. Our waters become toxic, and emotionally healthy people intuitively know it's time to leave.

Likewise, the less transparent we become in our leadership, blocking out the light, the more toxic our waters become. Pope Francis recently raised a caution about the future of the church, stating, "The evil spirit prefers a peaceful church, without risks, a business church, an easy church, in the comfort of warmth, lukewarm. When the church is lukewarm, tranquil, everything organized, there are no problems, look where the deals are," he stated, arguing that evil enters the church "through the pocket."[23]

While I may not always agree with Pope Francis's theology, I do agree with his caution. When we start to run our churches, and other organizations, like some sort of everyday business, we forget who and whose we are. We start to think only of what is good for the bottom line or what will keep more people happily in the pews. We stop talking about our values, and we make decisions in small groups, behind closed doors. The light from above is blocked out more and more, until nothing can live in our waters. If we want our communities to thrive, if we want to still be a part of Christ's living waters, it's our job to make sure that the waters stay clear.

CLEANING UP OUR COMMUNITIES

I know of several churches that have an important rule: before you can serve in any kind of leadership in the church, including on any committee, you first must do your own work. Would-be leaders must engage in self-reflection, including examining their life story, relationship with God, and ways in which they interact with others. Congregations offer different methods of doing this work, but they insist upon it for anyone who wants to lead. If a person refuses, they are still welcome to be an active member of the church, but they are presumed to have self-selected out of church leadership.

The benefit of this model is that only people who are willing to be self-reflective, and be honest about themselves and what might influence their reactions, end up leading the church. Those self-reflective people help the community to become self-reflective as well. This is why the work of discerning who should be a leader is so essential. It's sometimes even better to let a position go unfilled than to have anxiety about a blank spot and rush to fill it with someone who has not done their own work.

Church and ministry settings that are thoughtful about the people they put in leadership can begin to influence their entire congregational culture in a relatively short amount of time. Leaders who are capable of honesty and who can see God at work in their own life can better withstand fear and anxiety. They will help their communities navigate through crises without losing their bearings.

It is also necessary to find leaders who understand that their position is not a reward, but a calling. In recovery circles we have a tradition that we point to regularly: "Our leaders are but trusted servants; they do not govern."[24] We proclaim that there is "one ultimate authority—a loving God." Group leaders, from the local to national level, are in positions of service. They are no more important than the person walking into their first meeting ever.

I often wish that churches would internalize that lesson. Whether we are referring to lay leaders, local pastors, regional leaders, or denominational staff, our leaders are there to point toward God, not to take God's place. Leaders who are self-reflective and integrated will resist the urge to become the focus of attention and will instead take seriously the work of equipping the people of God. Leaders who do not do this work become celebrities at best, and seriously dangerous influences at worst. The destruction that narcissistic leaders have wrought in communities of faith is incalculable.

Worthy leaders will also be able to lead their community in having honest conversations. They will welcome checks on their leadership, invite opposing opinions, and be open to change. They will look for buy-in around new ideas, believing that the community's voice matters. They will understand that sometimes dissent in communities is necessary and even healthy. In fact, they will understand that one should never trust a community of faith that does not allow dissent.

In this way, too, even if you are not in a position of leadership, you must be willing to step forward when you see something amiss. This may not make you many friends, but it will allow you to maintain your integrity. To take your community seriously, to truly love it, is to be willing to tell it when it is wrong. To fail to do so is just one more example of enabling. We must love our communities of connection enough to hold them accountable.

INSTITUTIONAL AMENDS

In recovery groups there are times when the group itself will engage in a corporate fourth step. Members will gather together to "make a searching and fearless inventory" of themselves. They will tell the truth about what is happening in the group, look at the ways they have gone off course, and then turn to God for help in making things right again. This is not a process of blame, but rather of every member of the group taking responsibility to figure out how to be a better community together.

Contrast that to what happens in many churches. How often has one person—a pastor, or a committee member, or maybe just the guy who asks a lot of questions every annual meeting—been blamed? What would it be like to take a "searching and fearless moral inventory" of our church, and to look for a way forward? Many church conflicts might be addressed before the crisis point.

On a more serious level, the community might also be able to see the places where it too needs to make amends. On a recent visit with the United Church of Canada, I was struck by the repeated corporate remembrance of the church's role in the mistreatment of First Nations people. During one worship service the liturgist read prayers as pictures of First Nations children in religious residential schools were projected on the screen. The liturgist stopped repeatedly for us to intone in confession, "What have we done? What have we done?"

The history of the church in the North American context is one of an institution that has participated in a great many social evils. We have spread white supremacist, sexist, homophobic, and transphobic ideologies. We have hurt a great many people, directly and indirectly. Our legacy continues to inform the wider public perception around a great deal of social issues.

While we must be more than a sum of our failures, we must also be willing to learn from our failures. We must be able to tell the truth about communal histories and, even if we were not even alive at the time of the injustice, be willing to make amends to those who have been hurt in our communities' names.

As we move into the next section, this willingness to do the hard work of saying we are sorry will be essential. We cannot hope to be allies, or to intersect with others, while we are still not willing to look at our past and be honest. When a community is at its best, it can be an incredibly powerful influence in the lives of others, and it can be powerfully influenced by others. We can never be at our best, though, without being honest about who we have been.

INTERSECTING

One of the reasons it's so important for a community to do its internal work before going outside of itself is because we have the potential to do real harm. Even when we have the best of intentions, what we don't know can hurt not only us, but others. For communities of faith this can be especially acute. We are sometimes in such a hurry to do the right thing that we rush in without thinking about how we might cause harm.

I'll give you an example. When I lived in Vermont, the community was hit by a devastating flash flood. Entire buildings were washed away by an overflowing river, and we were left needing to rebuild. Immediately afterward people who lived outside of the community wanted to help. They began to organize food and clothing drives, and they claimed that they would drive up the next day to start helping us rebuild. The only problem was this wasn't the help we needed.

On top of this, many roads into town had been washed out, leaving very narrow and treacherous mountain passageways that needed to be preserved for emergency vehicles. When first responders begged people from out of town not to use the roads, they didn't listen. They drove on them, putting us all at further risk and adding more people into a small community that had limited space. I do not question that these were good people who wanted to help, but their actions actually hurt us.

So much of what it means to be in community with others is to learn to listen well. When our communities reach out in new ways, we have to carry this same ethic with us. Too often we seek to help, or to be allies, without asking what the other actually needs from us. We end up putting our own feelings and needs first by trying to assuage our guilt, wanting to be helpful, or needing assurance that we are good allies.

To do truly intersectional work we have to be willing to be transformed in the process. This is not about saving other people; this is about working with other people that we might create a more just world together. This work is too important to do without first doing our personal work and our communal work.

For those of us who hope to be allies to communities that have experienced oppression, this is crucial. Every movement needs good allies who can lend support and carry the message to the places the oppressed cannot go. For the LGBTQ community to be granted more of our civil rights, for instance, we needed, and still need, strong allies who could walk into the offices of their pastors and members of Congress and advocate for us.

It is when allies forget that they are there as support that things get tricky. A good ally knows that the struggle is not ultimately about them. Too often, though, that gets forgotten. Well-meaning white people might dominate a discussion about racism, a straight Christian might use a gay pride parade as a moment to "apologize" for the homophobia of the church, or a man might interrupt a woman describing her experiences of sexism with a reassurance that he is different. In each case, the allies make themselves the center of attention, thereby displacing the people who should be at the center.

When we have a chance to intersect, to work together with new communities and coalitions, we have to take it seriously enough to bring our most honest, integrated, and open selves. Enough pain has been caused by irresponsible people and groups without us contributing to it. If we want to be good allies, as individuals and as communities, we have to continually check our motives and methods; we have to let the ones most impacted by any particular struggle for justice take the lead. This means passing the microphone instead of taking it ourselves, elevating other voices over our own, and recognizing the privileges that we carry and remembering those privileges at every turn.

The formation of community is continual. We wrestle with our values, we open our doors to new people, we elevate worthy leadership, and we learn from our mistakes. Our communities define us, challenge us, and empower us to create real change. When our communities are strong in these ways, we are better for belonging to them. The work of recovery—and the work of resistance—are never solo projects, and the work of building better communities is never done.

SIX | INVESTED

TRANSFORMED AND TRANSFORMING

There's a truth about the twelve steps that you don't learn until you are almost done: you're never done. The truth hits you right around step nine, when you think you are leaving the hardest part behind. You've told yourself the truth, reconnected with God, come to know yourself, and reconciled with others. You've done the work, and you're on the home stretch. Then you hit the last three steps, and you realize that there's a whole journey left in front of you, and it won't end this side of heaven.

Steps ten through twelve are sometimes called "maintenance steps." These are the daily attitudes and practices that make recovery a lifelong journey. It is telling that members of twelve-step groups do not refer to themselves as "recovered alcoholics" or "recovered addicts" but as people who are "recovering." This should feel familiar to people of Christian faith. We understand that following Christ is a lifelong process of committing and recommitting ourselves to the journey. This is what it means to be a disciple, a student and follower of Christ. We try to grow in our faith and to act in the world in ways that glorify God.

The good news is that this is not a bleak future. Dietrich Bonhoeffer writes in *The Cost of Discipleship* these words: "Only Jesus Christ, who bids us follow him, knows the journey's end. But we do know that it will be a road of boundless mercy. Discipleship means joy."[25] Recovery, also, can be joy.

Recovery and discipleship are not the same thing, but they are two journeys that may be taken together and that complement one another well. These journeys are marathons, not sprints, demanding our continual attention and involvement. Both require a willingness to keep putting one foot in front of the other, day after day. Both expect us to choose never-ending transformation over spiritual stagnation. Both take work, but both can bring with them deep and abiding meaning and peace.

Both are also continually threatened by our reluctance to keep moving forward. The last three steps offer us a way to keep moving, a compass for our travels. The first of these lifelong practices is step ten: "Continued to take personal inventory and when we were wrong promptly admitted it." Many people in recovery take time each night to think through their day. Reviewing it from morning to evening, we look at our actions and find the places where we have felt joy and gratitude. Going a step further, we also look at what didn't turn out quite how we hoped. We try to figure out if we had a part in those things and, if we did, how to make it right.

There's a recovery phrase that's useful here: "keeping your own side of the street clean." It is not our job to clean up what others need to clean up for themselves (in fact, we can wreak serious havoc by doing so), but it is our responsibility to make sure others don't have to do our work. We don't "pass the buck" on to others. We are willing to continue to reflect on our own actions and to take steps to change things when needed. We are also willing to say "I'm sorry" when we mess up . . . and no matter how many years we have spent in recovery, we will still mess up regularly.

This process is not one of daily self-flagellation. It is simply continuing to reflect on who and whose we are and how we want to act in the world as a result. You should feel better about yourself, not worse. No matter what setbacks and missteps are in your path, you are still heading the right way, and you are still loved wildly by God. Reflecting on how things are going, and taking the steps to fix what isn't working, will only make the journey better.

CONSCIOUS CONTACT

There's a story about Solomon, the king who followed his father David to the throne. David is revered beyond measure for his courage, power, and greatness, but he's also remembered for the enormity of his mistakes. This is a man who had the husband of a woman he lusted after put on the front lines of battle so that he would die. This was also a man whose sons fought him, and one another, for power. When the unlikely Solomon was chosen to assume his role, he knew he had big shoes to fill, but he also had been a witness to the big mistakes his father had made. He knew that leaders are fallible.

What he did next is why we most remember Solomon. We are told that God appeared in a dream and asked Solomon what he wanted. While some kings might have asked for money, a long reign, or absolute power, Solomon asked for only one thing: wisdom. "Give me wisdom and knowledge so I can lead this people," Solomon asked, "because no one can govern this great people of yours without your help" (2 Chron. 1:10). God, pleased that Solomon asked for a blessing that would help him lead other people rather than help himself, blessed Solomon with wisdom and much more.

Of great importance to the parallel journeys of recovery and discipleship is our continued connection to God. Even the most seasoned and wise Christian can feel far away from God's presence, and even the person with decades of sobriety will wonder where their Higher Power is at times. What keeps both on the right path is their willingness to remain open to God's guidance. I believe that this is in many ways the same thing as seeking wisdom. God's wisdom helps us to engage this world well, and to transform it for the better.

Step eleven reads: "Sought through prayer and meditation to improve our conscious contact with God as we understood [God], praying only for knowledge of [God's] will for us and the power to carry that out."[26] What I love about this step is how open-ended it remains. While the step suggests prayer and meditation, those are broad categories contingent entirely on how we understand God and how we define prayer and meditation. I have always understood this to mean that however you best encounter God in any given time is good.

There have been times in my life where God has felt particularly close. Prayer has felt effortless and continuous, and I have intuitively seemed to know the next right step. There have also been times when God has felt completely obscured, doubt has surrounded me, and I've been hard pressed to do more than mumble a half-hearted Serenity Prayer. The beauty of step eleven is that in neither of those instances was I doing it more "right" than in the other. All that counts is that I was doing my best to remain connected to God and to try to figure out what God wanted for me to do next.

We sometimes disregard the importance of spiritual discernment. Faced with major decisions we too often default to business mode, weighing pros and cons on spreadsheets instead of engaging in prayer, meditation, and reflection, especially in community. The Holy Spirit's nudges may go unfelt, especially if we are in a hurry. There is too much noise in the world, and often it blocks out what we are supposed to hear. We start to mistake the loudest and most self-assured voices as the voice of God. If we really want to be spiritual people, though, listening to the Holy Spirit matters. Learning how to do that deliberately and regularly is the best training.

Some twelve-step groups will hold what they call "11th Step Meetings." These are specially structured to allow participants time and space to find God. Each looks a little different; some might begin with a prayer and then invite the meeting into silence so each member may pray or meditate. Others will sit around a lit candle, spending time first in quiet reflection and then in sharing what they heard in the silence. The point is to create a supportive and safe space for people to be intentional about their spiritual growth.

It is in our spiritual growth that wisdom comes. Like Solomon, we can choose what will be a priority in our life. We can decide to focus on the pursuit of power or riches, or we can instead seek what will make us wise. The guidance and direction that we receive is the solid rock that we will depend upon, especially in times that require moral courage. Our willingness to grow more each day, engaging more deeply with God, is what will give us the depth needed to resist fear and threats.

Bravery without wisdom is often just self-destruction. True courage comes from discernment that makes us root our actions in something greater than ourselves. For people who would follow Christ, this is in the Holy Spirit's continuing direction to us. We root ourselves in the strength that it can provide. Any courageous action we, or our communities, would take is worth doing the work of good discernment, of asking God for a little bit of wisdom.

LEADING LIVES OF GRATITUDE

It is spiritual wisdom that also brings us into awareness of our gratitude. While gratitude was an essential part of the faith I learned in seminary, something I understood at a basic level, it was not until I got sober that I really grasped what gratitude means. That's not a coincidence. Those of us who have faced ourselves at our worst, and who remember those times, also see most clearly the new life God has given to us. Grace is not a vague construct for us. Grace is what saved us.

In the Gospel of Luke there is a story about Jesus and ten lepers. Leprosy is a dreaded skin disease that was more common in Jesus's day. Because it was highly contagious, those who had it were ostracized. People tried to assign blame to those who contracted it, saying that it was punishment for sins. Religious authorities had the power to diagnose the condition and banish the sufferer. There were few things more dreaded that becoming a leper.

One day as Jesus was walking to Jerusalem ten lepers appeared and shouted to him, "Jesus, Master, have mercy on us" (Luke 17:13ff). Jesus healed all ten and told them to go and show the priests, who could then pronounce them cured. Nine of them took off right away for the village, but one did not. Overcome, he fell down at Jesus's feet and thanked him. He is the only one to choose the path of gratitude. This did not go unnoticed by Jesus, who asked, "Weren't ten healed? Where are the other nine?"

I never want to be the person who is given new life only to forget the one who gave it to me. I want to choose the grateful response, the one that is less concerned about going and getting my old life back than about saying "Thank you." I have so much in my life to be grateful for, including my sobriety. Looking back on my life, I can see where God has interceded for good and how God has transformed even the worst experiences. I do not believe that God ever wills us to suffer or to experience evil and hatred, but I do believe that God can help us to overcome these things and emerge on the other side with new strength and wisdom.

Gratitude is an important part of recovery culture. Early in sobriety I kept hearing people say, "A grateful heart will never drink." I was so angry that I had to get sober that I had no idea what anyone was so grateful for in those days. They sounded like broken records, repeating trite slogans. One day someone who had been sober a long time even suggested I write something called a "gratitude list." The idea was to sit down with pen and paper and list every single thing in my life for which I was grateful.

I had a lot of suggestions about what she could do with her gratitude list.

For some reason, probably because I didn't know what else to do, I tried it. I would have tried just about anything else to feel good, so why not give this a shot? I sat down and started with the easy things: I have a place to live, I have enough to eat, I have a job. Then I started to go deeper: I have family who love me, I have good friends, I have an education and skills. And then something happened: I have my sobriety, I have a future, I have . . . hope.

Hope is an amazing thing. Too often we live without it. When we learn to look at the world with gratitude, though, and when we are able to see all that we have by God's grace, we start to see possibilities where previously we saw only barriers. On days when I feel hopeless or defeated, I still do this exercise, and through gratitude I still always get to a place of hope.

I now understand what it means to say, "A grateful heart will never drink." The closer I stay to my gratitude, the more aware I am of how much I have to lose. I have been given blessing upon blessing. If I ever return to drinking, I will lose it all. But it's not just the fear of loss that motivates me; it's the profound desire to tell God that I am grateful and to embrace the possibilities that hope has given to me. I want to live my life as my "thank you" to God.

But if you don't believe a theologian about the benefits of gratitude, listen to a scientist. Dr. Robert A. Emmons, a psychology professor at the University of California-Davis, states that gratitude "can lower blood pressure, improve immune function and facilitate more efficient sleep. Gratitude reduces lifetime risk for depression, anxiety, and substance abuse disorders, and is a key resiliency factor in the prevention of suicide."[27]

Emmons hypothesizes that this is because gratitude "allows individuals to celebrate the present and be an active participant in their own lives."[28] Much as the Serenity Prayer states, when we know that we have some agency in our own lives, and we know that we can ask God for the "courage to change the things we can," we start to have real hope. This is not about just wishing for something better; this is about looking at our lives, seeing that change is possible, and choosing to be actively engaged with God in creating that change. We are not helpless; we are powerfully supported by a God who has already loved us through so much. Our job is to simply learn how to say "thank you."

KNOWING OUR PURPOSE

Gratitude is our compass. It helps us find our true north and turns our hearts to it. It is also our motivator. It shows us a path, and it gives us the strength and endurance we need to travel that path. I've often said that the best indicator that a church is dying is that the people in it cannot tell you about God's grace in their own lives. By contrast, members of spiritually thriving churches can not only can tell you how God has interceded for good in their lives, but they also are people who want to say "thank you" to God with everything that they do. In short, gratitude is essential to our sense of purpose.

It is my belief that in order to truly "rise," to live out resurrection in this world, we must know our purpose. For me, and I believe for many, that purpose is to live a life of gratitude to God for the new life that I have received.

The best way I know to show gratitude to God is to live as a resurrection person in this world. I live as an example of what God's grace has done. I also live not just for myself but for others, all of whom God loves just as much as me. I want God to be able to use me as a tool, one that can help others to find their own way to new life, and one of many whom God can use to help this whole world to rise.

When we started this section of the book, we talked about Erikson and his stages of life. We talked about identity, about knowing who we are, and we talked about intimacy and about knowing whose we are too. My hope is that by this point of the book you have found new understandings of those two important questions. We are at the halfway point, and we are about to make a turn toward Erikson's next big step: generativity.

Erikson believed that when we have reached this stage of development, we become concerned with others, particularly the next generation (a word that shares its root with "generativity"). Erikson wrote "Generativity is primarily the interest in establishing and guiding the next generation," either through raising our own children or through, "other forms of altruistic concern and of creativity."[29]

While Erikson was privileging parenting here, I believe that generativity could be understood in a much broader way. I understand generativity not as parenting, and especially not as paternalism, but as genuine concern for others, especially for those who are traveling the same paths that we once traveled ourselves. In a way, generativity is about our willingness to jump into the same holes that others have jumped in for us and to help the next in line to find their way out.

For Erikson, the greatest threat to generativity was the threat of "stagnation." He writes, "Individuals who do not develop generativity often begin to indulge themselves as if they were their own one and only child."[30] Put more broadly, they become selfish. They are like the nine healed lepers who run back to town to get their old life back, not like the one who cannot help but say "thank you."

THE NEXT HALF OF THE JOURNEY

Everything about my faith, everything about my recovery, has taught me that I need to find a way to be generative and concerned with others, including those who may come long after me. In a few pages we will be moving into the second half of this book, and we will be moving away from the more explicit discussion of recovery concepts and into a discussion of what it means to resist. It would be wrong to think that we are leaving recovery behind, though.

You will find the concepts from this section echoed in what is to come. In part II we will explore how to be generative in this world through the lens of actively resisting oppression and evil by choosing to participate in resurrection instead. This is still the work of recovery, and it is work made more possible because of the journey you have taken in this section. It is also the work of the final, and most unending, of the twelve steps.

Step twelve reads: "Having had a spiritual awakening as the result of these steps, we tried to carry this message to alcoholics, and to practice these principles in all our affairs." This is the "service" step, the one that mandates that we do generative work in the world. Service is at the heart of twelve-step programs. Members give back in some way, whether it's making coffee for the meeting or being a sponsor to newcomers. It's an inseparable part of recovery.

It's also, truth be told, just a little bit selfish. Ask any of us who have been sober for a while what service means to us, especially the support of newcomers, and sooner or later we'll tell you this: It helps me stay sober too. Somewhere in the midst of telling our own stories, sitting with people who are just quitting drinking, or visiting rehab facilities or hospitals, we are given the chance to remember how far we have been brought by grace. We are also given the blessing of being useful.

Serving others means that we realize our blessings are not just for ourselves. Often on social media I see someone post about a new house or car with the hashtag #blessed. It seems that some believe God gives us material things for our own benefit. The truly blessed, though, receive the kind of gifts that they cannot help but share. People in recovery understand that we have been blessed not for ourselves, but for others. We have been saved from destruction, and for others.

Recovery, like faith, requires us to serve one another. If we fail to do so, we will surely become as stagnant as dead water.

In part II, each chapter's title ends in "ing," the suffix that suggests doing. This is by design. This is when we begin the generative work that is not so unlike twelve-step work. This is how we choose to engage a world that is so in need of recovery of every kind imaginable, including that which a twelve-step meeting cannot even begin to address. The good news is that we have new tools we can use in this work.

As we end this part, remember for a moment what you have had to overcome. There has been some pharaoh who wanted you dead and who drove you out in the wilderness. There is something in your life that you have tried to run from just as surely as Jonah ran from Nineveh, but that still held you prisoner in a cell as bleak the belly of a whale. There is something with which you have had to wrestle just as surely as Jacob did with God. There is something that has had you down at the bottom of a steep hole, looking up with no way to escape.

But there is also someone who, when you were alone in the city, a prodigal who longed for home, stood on the road waiting for you to come back. There is someone who has been running with you, waiting for you to turn back around. There is someone who jumps into the deepest hole, someone who knows the way out. And there is someone who has loved you into wholeness and who only wants for you to be the one who stays around to say "thank you."

There is someone who has helped you to recover your truest and best self and who walks with you even still. Our purpose rests in that Someone, whom I call "God," and in the hope and promise of resurrection. Resurrection is not something that just happened on that Easter morning two thousand years ago. It happens every day, and it is available to each of us. I've spent my fair share of time down in the tombs, but I have found my way out and into new life. Because of the grace of God, I know what it is to rise and to recover.

We have all been given this grace, and now we get to decide how to respond. I choose, or at least try my best to choose, gratitude. Saying "thank you" to God is my purpose in life. It is the way that I thank God for my resurrection, the way I choose to continue to rise in Christ.

And it is also the reason why I choose to resist.

PART TWO

Resist

The Courage to Change the World

SEVEN | PERSEVERING

HERE I STAND?

In 1521, four years after he had nailed his *95 Theses* to the door of the Wittenberg church, Martin Luther stood in front of the Diet of Worms. His teachings had set Europe on fire, and the Diet, a sort of tribunal, had been called by Emperor Charles the Fifth so that Luther could explain himself. For a guy who had been an ordinary monk just a few short years before, this was intimidating stuff.

The story of what happened next is usually told in triumphant tones, with Luther loudly and confidently defending his teachings, ending with a defiant shout of "Here I stand! I can do none other!" Luther is remembered five hundred years later as the fearless hero who faced down an emperor and a powerful church, and kick-started the Protestant Reformation. Even now we who are faithful are encouraged to be courageous like Luther, unrelenting in the proclamation of our truth.

I wish I could be like that Luther. I'd love to be courageous all the time, and I'd like to think that I could face down empires. The reality is that I'm not so sure I would handle a summons to explain myself to the emperor anywhere near as well as he did. The good news, though, is that Luther probably didn't either.

Historians who research the Diet of Worms tell us that on the first day of the gathering, April 17, 1521, Luther comes in to defend himself. The leaders of the gathering, mostly his opponents, bring him into the room, point to a collection of Luther's books and papers, and ask him if the books are his. They then ask if he is ready to renounce the heresies contained in them.

So, this is the big moment, right? This is when Luther jumps to his feet and shouts his famous line? Here is where he stands!

It isn't. In fact, nothing even close. Instead, Luther says he needs some time to think about his answer. He doesn't even say, "Yes, I wrote those." Some historical accounts say that Luther speaks so softly that people can't even hear his response. That night he goes back to his room, thinks, prays, talks with friends, and comes back the next day to face the court. This time, he answers.

Luther says that these are indeed his books. He says that he cannot renounce what he wrote, because "If I now recant these, then, I would be doing nothing but strengthening tyranny."[31] And then he says something that is a matter of great debate. It likely begins like this, "My conscience is captive to the Word of God. I cannot and I will not recant anything, for to go against conscience is neither right nor safe. God help me. Amen." How it ended, though, depends on whom you ask.

Legend says this is when Luther declared, "Here I stand! I can do none other!" In reality there probably was no triumphant, movie-worthy moment. Sometime in the aftermath, as the story was told and retold, Luther was transformed from a nervous writer to a fearless fighter who bravely proclaimed his belief to the emperor. It is a great story. I love the image of the little guy standing up to the powers that be. But it's the real story, the one of an ordinary monk who was probably scared to death, the one who states his truth and says "God help me" that I like even more.

STANDING FAST, STANDING AGAIN

I recently saw a picture of the audience at a Nazi rally. In a packed arena, rows upon rows of people are looking toward the stage, raising their arms out in front of them in a Nazi salute. One man is not. Arms crossed defiantly in front of him, he looks on, unmoved. When I saw the picture, someone had circled this man, and written the words "be this guy" beneath it.

I would love to be that guy. I want to be so unafraid that I am always willing to do the right thing. I want to stand in an arena and refuse to worship a false god. I'd like to believe that if I had been alive at the time, I would have done just that. I'd also like to believe that I would have marched across the Selma bridge with Dr. King, been a conductor on the Underground Railroad, thrown tea into the Boston Harbor, shouted "Here I stand" at the emperor, and stayed awake all night with Jesus, too.

My ego wants me to believe that, of course, I would do all of those things. The realistic part of me knows that it's a whole lot harder than that. True resistance, like recovery, always costs something, and so resistance, like recovery, always requires moral courage. The objective of the first part of this book was to help us to think about what it means to be morally courageous in our own lives and in our communities of support. The objective of the second part is to apply those lessons to the work of resistance so that we can all get just a little closer to being "that guy."

As I write about the concept of "resistance," I am aware of the way this term has been politicized following the 2016 presidential election in the United States. While much of what I say here may well have resonance with those who identify with that movement, the concept I'm discussing is much broader in its reach and power than what is being discussed in this particular time and place in history. In particular, this is about resistance as a Christian value, one upon which the faith depends in every age. This is about our baptismal vows to resist oppression and evil wherever we might find them.

Once again, we return to the root of a word for greater clarity. Our English word "resist" comes from the Latin *resistere*. *Sistere* translates as "stand," and *re* as "back," "again," or "remain." Resistance literally means to "stand again" or "remain standing." To be people of resistance is to be standing-fast, or steadfast, people. We remain standing when it comes to our principles, and we stand again when we are knocked down because of them.

To put it in more inclusive terms, we rise, and we rise again, and again, and again. We become resurrection people who cannot help but to do so. The really good news is that those of us who have been through a journey of recovery, a journey of resurrection, know how to do this well. We have been made for this. Resistance is resurrection, and resurrection is resistance.

One of the communities where I spent my early sobriety was Provincetown, Massachusetts. Provincetown is, per capita, the home to more LGBTQ people than anywhere else. It also has a large and excellent recovery community. In my first years of recovery, these were the people who loved me and taught me what it meant to live resurrection.

Many of them knew firsthand, and in more ways than one, what it meant to be in the tombs and then find that new life was possible. In the 1980s, as the AIDS crisis raged unaddressed by the government and public sentiment was often negative to those with HIV, the gay community was especially ravished. It was not uncommon for someone to receive a diagnosis and die within months. In the early 1990s when I first came out, advertisements for "viaticals," an option to sell a life insurance policy for cash, could be found in every gay magazine. Buying the life insurance policy of a young person with HIV or AIDS was, unfortunately, a good investment for companies that wanted quick cash.

The HIV-positive person, who now had a little bit of money to survive on, could make plans about living out their last months. For many in cities like New York or Boston, Provincetown became an idyllic, gay-friendly location to spend their last months. They could come out to the very tip of Cape Cod, be safe, and get some small amount of comfort and joy before they died.

But here's the kicker . . . in the mid-1990s, what is now known as "the cocktail" changed HIV treatment. New drugs were combined in a way that drastically improved the health of people with HIV. All of a sudden, people who had been told they had months to a year or two to live now might have decades. The life they thought would soon be over now was full of promise and potential. Instead of accepting imminent death, they now had the chance to resist it.

That was good news, but for some of the newly hopeful who were also addicted to alcohol and drugs, a condition exacerbated by previous hopelessness, it also meant choosing whether or not to get clean and sober. They had expected to die, and now they had the chance to live. What would their choice be? To stay in the tombs? Or to rise, and resist?

I am personally grateful that so many of these men chose the path of resistance. They turned away from addiction and claimed new life. As a result, by the time I came to town, many of these men had over a decade of sobriety. They knew what it was to choose to live in the face of death, and they were ready to help the next generation to do the same. Both through their work in the recovery community, and through their tireless efforts to advance LGBTQ rights through the next decades, they chose a path of service. They were doing generative work, in the best sense of the word. They helped to save my life, and the work that they have done will save the lives of those who come long afterward. They taught me what it means to rise, and they taught me what it means to resist.

CHOOSING TO STAY

HIV-positive gay folks with addiction issues were not exactly a beloved part of the national landscape in the 1990s. It is not an overstatement to say that some would not have cared had these people died. Some particularly callous people may even have hoped for it. But instead, the HIV folks lived; not only that, they often thrived. This was in a world where Ellen Degeneres lost her career for coming out, and gay marriage was so unimaginable that not even gay folks believed it would ever happen. To simply live, and to live happily at that, was real resistance.

In classical Reformed theology there is a concept called "the perseverance of the saints." John Calvin, another of the founders of the Reformation along with Luther, was also the father of the Reformed tradition that includes the modern-day United Church of Christ and Presbyterian Churches, among others. He believed that once a person had experienced a "regeneration," in which the Holy Spirit acted in their life, it was impossible for them to ever be separated from God.

Regeneration, for Calvin, was a conversion. Earlier we talked about "conversion" as literally meaning "to turn around." Recovery is a profound form of conversion, one in which I believe the Holy Spirit is actively involved. I believe that once a person has any experience of regeneration, even if the path that follows includes stumbling blocks and setbacks, they will remain aware of the love of God at some level. The difference between Calvin and me, though, is that I believe this regeneration is available to all and that, if we look back at our lives, we will realize that we all have in some way already experienced it.

Calvin wrote, "No one can travel so far that [they do] not make some progress each day. So let us never give up. Then we shall move forward daily in the Lord's way. And let us never despair because of our limited success. Even though it is so much less than we would like, our labor is not wasted when today is better than yesterday!"[32] This is what Calvin means by the "perseverance of the saints." Once we are on a spiritual path, God will not let us turn back—at least not for long. We continue to be drawn forward, as surely as the prodigal son was drawn home. The journey continues for as long as we are alive, and even into the world to come.

For those of us who have wrestled with what it means to survive in this world, this is a call to keep going. The perseverance of the saints, in modern terms, could be described as the persistence of the survivors. To return to the e. e. cummings statement from earlier, "To be nobody-but-yourself—in a world which is doing its best day and night to make you everybody else—means to fight the hardest battle which any human being can fight; and never stop fighting."[33]

If you are in any way different from what society expects of you, or if you in any way challenge the systems that are in place, you can be seen as a threat. The reality is that sometimes the most evil and deadly parts of this world want you to hate yourself. In fact, they may want you to hate yourself to death. And when you don't comply with their death wish, they will hate you even more. To choose to simply survive is nothing less than an act of profound resistance to the forces of destruction that surround us every day. To persist, to commit yourself to the continued journey toward wholeness, is nothing less than spiritual perseverance.

Comedian Margaret Cho, describing her own struggle with suicidal ideation and the decision to continue to live in a world filled with injustice and oppression, wrote, "I have chosen to stay and fight."[34] There is so much in this world that is unfair and wrong. If you are a person who has experienced injustice or abuse or who has to deal with the bigotry of the world on a daily basis, life itself can sometimes feel exhausting. In the worst moments, when it seems like nothing will change or get better, we might begin to consider drastic options.

I get that. In my twenties, before I got sober, I struggled with whether or not this world was worth living in, at least for me. What kept me alive was a belief that God was still with me on this journey and would help me to persevere. In some small place, I carried hope, and that's what helped me to survive. I know that others did not survive, and I am in no way saying that they were less beloved by God, that they failed, or that they were not loved enough by those who loved them. This world is a cruel place for so many, and to put the blame on the victims of that cruelty is unjust. I was somehow able to hold that hope in the darkest hours and to choose the path of resistance that comes from survival.

This is not to say that I, or anyone, should deny the reality of what we have faced. Even the resurrected Christ still carried the scars of his crucifixion on his body. It is to say that even in the face of the worst of what the world can do, we can choose another way. We can choose not to leave this world, either literally or simply through a refusal to participate in the betterment of it. We can choose instead to persist as an act of hope and as a witness of a better way for those to come. We can choose to "stay and fight."

THE NOT-SO-FEARLESS RESISTANCE

To choose to persist does take courage. That has always been true. When Martin Luther was called to the Diet of Worms he could have chosen the way of least resistance. He could have recanted of his teachings and walked away. Instead, after he gave his defense, he left the Diet before it was done, and he was declared an outlaw. In the custom of the times, that meant that anyone could have killed him, which was really not an ideal situation. His friends arranged to have him "kidnapped" (he gave his permission first) and took him into hiding at Wartburg.

The "here I stand" legend probably sprang up soon afterward, embellished with each retelling, and preserved for the ages. Earlier I said that I like that "here I stand" story, but I love the real story even more. I think that's because I can identify with it. We all want to be courageous, but we all also grapple with fear. It's somehow comforting to know that Martin Luther didn't want to die anymore than we do.

In fact, the real story makes me respect Martin Luther's courage even more. He may have had an extraordinary mind, but he was a regular guy when it came to acts of heroism. His courage came not from his stoutness of heart, but from his belief that God was with him on the journey and that he just had to keep persevering. It would have been safer to repudiate his writings, but it wouldn't have been true. Ultimately, having to deny the love of God that he had come to know on his rocky journey was worse than the fear becoming an outlaw. All he could do was state his truth and then pray simply, "God help me."

Too often we equate courage with fearlessness, but the two are actually diametrically opposed. The courageous person does not lack fear; fear exists for them, but they somehow resist it. If someone lacks fear in the face of real danger then one of two things are true: they are either a sociopath, incapable of feeling real fear, or they have a death wish. Neither means that they are courageous.

To have real courage, to live and act in ways that are congruent with what your heart and soul know, is to learn to resist your fear enough to be able do the right thing. Fear takes our choices away, causing us to flee or to freeze. Courage thaws us and engages us in the struggle. Fear causes us to sabotage ourselves and to abandon our friends and neighbors. Courage makes us truly generative, strengthens us enough to stand up for others. Fear keeps us in the grave. Courage brings us out of the tombs.

Spreading fear is the primary tool of tyrants and bullies. They use our fear for our own futures and our fears of others to gain power. They prey on human vulnerability in order to impose immoral and unjust systems. Too often, even when we disagree with them, we collude with these systems through our own inaction, too afraid to really resist.

Courage is the ability to resist our own fear and to resist the fear spread by others. We hold faith in a God of resurrection who always remains close to those who persevere, and so through courageous solidarity we share that resurrection with others. We refuse to be intimidated into silence and complicity, choosing to place our ultimate faith not in earthly powers, but in the one who loved us first. Courage is nothing less than faith that knows where its true loyalties lie.

DANCING DEFIANCE

I sometimes ask my congregation this question when I preach: "What would you do if you were unafraid?" That is ultimately a question of faith. The real question is this: "What would you do if you believed in God's promise enough that you would not be intimidated by the negative messages of this world?" Some people who hear this question are inspired into action by it. Others are deeply unsettled. When we have to face our own capacity for courage, we learn important things about our faith life, and sometimes it's not comforting.

One of the biggest lessons I've learned in recovery is that I don't want to let myself be intimidated anymore. I don't want to feel powerless in this world, and I don't want to make choices that don't feel good to me because I'm afraid to do the right thing. The gift that recovery has given me is the realization that much of the worst that can happen to me has already happened. I've been to rock bottom. I've rebuilt my life on a solid foundation. In many ways I've never had more to lose.

The counterintuitive part of that equation is not that I have become more cautious, more reluctant to do anything to risk to life I've built, but that I have become more courageous. Recovery has taught me that I am a survivor, and I have been built for resistance. I already know that the bedrock of my life—who I am, whose I am, and what my values are as a result—can never be destroyed so long as I remain true to it. Conversely, if I allow myself to be so intimidated that I compromise those values, they will crumble beneath me, and I will lose everything.

The capacity of survivors to resist is inspiring to me. In June of 2016, the day after the devastating mass shooting at the Pulse nightclub, a bar that catered primarily to the LGBTQ community, I flew to Orlando with several friends. We were there to serve as trauma chaplains for those who needed it. We spent the next few days talking to survivors and to family and friends of victims. Forty-nine people had been killed by a man whose hatred of LGBTQ people was documented. The devastation and pain were everywhere.

The shooting had taken place on the bar's Latin night, and many members of Orlando's tight-knit Latinx LGBTQ community had been present. A few nights later we crowded into another Orlando gay bar for the first Latin night since the shootings. Walking in, I became aware that almost everyone in that room had lost either a friend or family member or knew someone who had.

Alice Walker once wrote that "resistance is the secret of joy."[35] If that is true, it explains what I saw that night. No one was denying the truth of what had happened. There was anger, and there were tears. Grief was displayed openly, and pain was palpable. And yet, something else was happening too.

On the stage, and on the floor, people were dancing. Some had literally been caught in a hail of bullets days earlier, and here they were, all genders, and all sexual orientations, dancing the merengue as a drag queen declared from the stage that they were not going to let one man intimidate them. I have never seen people dance with more pain, and I have never seen people dance with more joy. The world had done its worse, and they were not cowering in fear. They were dancing their resistance. They were persevering as sure as any saint. If I have ever experienced a foretaste the kingdom of heaven, it was that night.

In the aftermath of the shooting, Orlando's gay newspaper, *Watermark*, carried these words on its cover: "You cannot silence us. You cannot destroy us. We are not going anywhere."[36] These were the right words for the moment, and they are the right words for any of us who would resist fear and work for change. We are survivors, and we will persevere, sometimes with fear and trembling, but with persistence at every step. And resistance will be our dance.

EIGHT | CHOOSING

WHEN LOYALTIES ARE TESTED

In 1933, a German man named Martin Niemöller was lending his support to an emerging national leader named Adolf Hitler. Niemöller had been awarded an Iron Cross, a distinguished German military decoration, for his service as a naval officer and submariner during World War I. He deeply loved his country and longed for national renewal during the hard years following Germany's defeat in World War I. Hitler, who was stirring passion in his fellow Germans, seemed to Niemöller like just the man who could lead such a renewal.

That might have been the end of the story for Niemöller had it not been for one thing: he was a Christian, and a pastor as well. Plenty of other German Christians had supported Hilter's ascent, including many pastors, so that was not unusual. Early on Niemöller even agreed with the anti-Semitic notions of the Nazi party. With time, though, Niemöller began to see the fallacies in Hitler's thought and to reject the bigotry and growing tyranny of the Nazi party.

This was a risky time for anyone to oppose the Third Reich, even in the church. The Nazi party was infiltrating the German Evangelical Protestant Church, a union of Reformed and Lutheran congregations, gaining power in church elections, and installing its own state-run Protestant Reich Church. Church youth movements were folded into the Hitler Youth. The Nazi swastika was superimposed on depictions of the cross. Pastors were pressured to dismiss much of the Hebrew Bible (known as the Old Testament to Christians), to downplay Jesus's Jewish identity and to proclaim that the Jewish people had killed Jesus. They were also told to extol the superiority of the Aryan race and to preach that other races were created inferior by God.

The Nazis did not want to control the church because of their religious faith. Many, like Joseph Goebbels, were outspoken in their anti-Christian beliefs. The Third Reich understood the strategic power of organized religion, however, and the influence they could exert over people of faith through the churches. There is a reason that tyrants often use the language of religion as a tool of their populist appeal, even today. By convincing people of faith that their beliefs support a particularly agenda, unscrupulous leaders can deceive the masses and harness the power of congregations keen to further God's realm.

In Germany the Nazis encountered far less resistance than we would hope in their takeover of the church. They even began to argue that other Christians, who did not support the state church, were not true Christians, thereby discrediting faithful dissenters. Before long the Nazi Party demanded that all pastors subscribe to the "Aryan paragraph," which stripped Jewish citizens, as well as others, of their rights and property. And that is where Pastor Martin Niemöller's crisis of loyalty finally began.

OUR ULTIMATE LOYALTY

Each of us carries within us conflicts of loyalty. We love God, but we do not love God alone. We may love our family, our friends, our country, our work, our political commitments, our alma maters, our favorite sports teams, or even our possessions. Love is not a bad thing. It binds us to one another, and it helps us to clarify our values. It is not love that is the problem, but love placed on the wrong things and in the wrong places. When we love what cannot and does not love us back, we waste our love, and we squander the best of ourselves.

For a Christian, our ultimate love, and our ultimate loyalty, must lie in God. Every other love and loyalty in our lives must be subject to that first commitment. Our love of our closest family and friends may be deep, and our loyalty fierce, but even those must be second to our love of, and loyalty to, God. This is not a rejection of our loved ones. This is simply an understanding that all we love comes from God, including one another. God's goodness is what creates every other goodness in the world.

Too often, though, we elevate what is not God into the place of God. This can be other human beings, but it can also be ideas and things. We can become so distracted by our love for another, or by our veneration of a leader or of our country, or by our pursuit of things like money or power, that we begin to worship them instead of God. When this happens, we lose sight of our ultimate love and loyalty. Put simply, we begin to forget "who" and "whose" we are.

This is called idolatry, and it is more dangerous than we know. The first two of the Ten Commandments warn us about this. The first, "I am the Lord thy God, . . . you shall have no other gods before me" is followed by "You shall not make for yourself an idol." These are the base requirements of what it means to love and follow God for both the Jewish and Christian faiths: know who God is, and don't let anything else become God for you.

That's often easier said than done. Though we may say the right things, we too often let what is not God take God's place. Often this is because in our desire for hope, and by our many fears, we are easily deceived. What can destroy us lies to us and tells us it is the answer, that it is from God. Whenever anything would try to take the place of God, we should immediately be on alert, because those who truly love God would never try to take God's place.

The German Christians who allowed Naziism to enter their church did so because they in some way believed that Hitler could save them. They put their faith not in Christ, but in the shallow hopes offered to them by a man who spread hate and destruction. Most German Christians were not threatened, at least immediately, by Hitler. They were not facing the reality of concentration camps or certain death. They were not personally impacted by the evil he had in store for so many. Hitler would be the salvation of the Germans who were like them.

In their acceptance of Naziism's creeping influence they put their hopes in one who was not God, and as a result they gave their loyalty to him too. As Christ taught, a house divided cannot stand. Everyone should have opposed the rise of the Nazi party, but Christians in particular, with our clear call to reject anything or anyone who tries to take God's place, should have been the most vocal opponents. In retrospect, it's hard to imagine how this happened.

The rise of Hitler is a very extreme and concrete example of idolatry in action, but the shifting of our loyalties is often far more insidious. If anything, we should look at the German Christians and realize that if they could be deluded so easily despite the very clear contrast between wrong and right, so can we. In fact, in the absence of such clear evil, it is even easier. The challenge for us becomes learning to see when our loyalties are in the wrong places, and then shifting them back to center on God and God's desire for the world. We must learn to love in the right order, not allowing our loyalties to be split, but growing in our allegiance to the only One who loved us first and who continues to love us above all.

There is a well-known passage from the book of Joshua. Having fled the pharoah's oppression, crossed the Red Sea, and wandered in the wilderness, the Hebrew people finally arrive in the promised land. Calling the community together, Joshua recounts all that God has done for them and then issues a challenge: "So now, revere the Lord. Serve God honestly and faithfully. Put aside the gods that your ancestors served beyond the Euphrates and in Egypt and serve the Lord. But if it seems wrong in your opinion to serve the Lord, then choose today whom you will serve. Choose the gods whom your ancestors served . . . but my family and I will serve the Lord" (Josh. 24:14–15 CEB).

A lot of people like to quote that passage. You can even buy mass-produced signs that say that, and nail one up in your living room. It's a lovely-sounding, family-focused sentiment. What we forget is that it is deeply dangerous. Joshua gives the people a choice. They can follow God, or they declare their loyalty to the gods they knew back in captivity. Joshua sets the example, though, making the decision that he will choose to serve God and to give God his first loyalty.

The choice is still ours today. We would like to think that we would not choose the gods of our captivity—but make no mistake, we still choose them every day. Deciding that we will leave our captors behind, giving our first loyalty only to God, is a revolutionary and countercultural act. It is saying that we choose a better way and refuse to allow anything the chance to steal our hope. It's a commitment that we will give our best service, and our best efforts, to the only one who truly deserves it. In the end, to declare your ultimate loyalty only to God is an act of resistance of the highest order.

WHAT WE MUST REJECT

As the Third Reich continued to rise to power and corrupt the church, a movement started to grow. Calling themselves the Confessing Church, a group of Christians began to challenge Hitler and his ideas. One of their greatest stands was in the German city of Barmen in 1934. Influenced heavily by theologian Karl Barth, who did most

RESIST | THE COURAGE TO CHANGE THE WORLD

of the writing, representatives from German Protestant churches drafted a document that outlined their rejection of Naziism and affirmed their loyalty to Christ above all.

The name "The Theological Declaration of Barmen" sounds pretty dry. Truth be told, even the document itself might read as a little stiff and academic at first glance. The ideas found within it, though, are anything but mundane. The gathering presented the confession as a call to the conscience of churches, exhorting them to listen: "Be not deceived by loose talk, as if we meant to oppose the unity of the German nation! Do not listen to the seducers who pervert our intentions . . . ! Try the spirit whether they are of God!"[37]

The writers go on to proclaim that the faith is "grievously imperiled" by the German Christian movement, and that "we may not keep silent." They then offer six truths, each of which directly contradicts Nazi teachings: Jesus Christ alone, and not the teachings of Hitler, is the one true Word of God. Jesus Christ alone, and not Hitler, is the only one to whom we belong. Jesus Christ alone, and not the message of the Nazi party, is the only message of our faith. Jesus Christ alone, and not Hitler, is the head of the church. Jesus Christ alone, and not the state, is to whom we answer. And Jesus Christ alone, and not Hitler, will be with us until the end of the age.[38]

With each of these truths, the Confessing Church struck a blow against the corrupted gospel of the German Christian Church. In a time of deep moral crisis, when the true teaching of Christ was being twisted into a tool of Nazi propaganda, they displayed the moral courage to tell the truth. They also displayed the courage to risk their own lives, as every one of those truths that they told was enough to get them arrested, imprisoned, and even killed.

By their actions, and by their commitment to resisting idolatry, they provided an example for their fellow Germans. They declared that the Gospel of Jesus Christ could not be reconciled with the beliefs of the Nazis. They made it clear that if one wished to be a Christian, they were going to have to make a choice between Jesus and Hitler. You could not give your loyalty to both.

To be truly loyal to something means that you have to be willing to reject something else. Just as a Christian in Germany could not also be loyal to the Nazi party, even today we must choose our ultimate loyalty if we want to follow Christ. This will sometimes mean that we have to stand up and speak against things we may have once dearly loved. Many of the Confessing Church members had been deeply patriotic Germans, some even serving in World War I, like Martin Niemöller. As much as they loved their country, though, they loved their God more. If being a patriotic German now meant that they had to also be Nazis, they could no longer give their loyalty to Germany.

The choices we make today as Christians are often less stark. That does not mean that our situation is not dangerous, though. For American Christians in particular, our faith is too often intertwined with patriotic fervor. Despite our Constitutional allegiance to separation of church and state, too often we confuse being a good American with being a good Christian, and vice versa. Politicians and political parties that use the enticement of Christian churches as a campaign strategy are particularly troublesome.

This is not to say that loving your country is a bad thing. Indeed, loyalty to "God and country" sounds like a virtuous idea. For a person of faith, though, that is only true if those loyalties are seen as hierarchical, with God above all. When one's country is asking you to act in ways that are contrary to your faith, or even simply to keep quiet as they do so, then you must be willing to declare your loyalty to your higher calling, and to resist.

The irony is that when we are loyal to our highest callings, we often are also bettering the other things and places to which we are loyal. When we are loyal to a God who loves us and who asks us to love our neighbors as ourselves, we may be forced to be voices of dissent in our countries, communities, and even in our churches. The good news is that dissent can be a sign of deep loyalty in and of itself. To truly love something, we must be willing not to collude with it when it is at its worst. Enabling that which we love to live down to its basest instincts is not loyalty at all, but an enabling of self-destruction.

FIRST THEY CAME . . .

Not long after Hitler's ascendance, Pastor Martin Niemöller had seen the error of his ways. His earlier support of Hitler, born from his love of his German homeland, had proven to be ill-advised. Hitler was now demanding that German pastors agree to the Aryan paragraph, which would later lead to the Nuremberg laws and the mass murder of millions. Niemöller began to realize the danger at hand for both his country and his faith.

Niemöller became the leader of the Pfarrernotbund, or Pastor's Emergency League. The League became the base of the Christian resistance to Naziism and was a major influence upon the gathering that would produce the Theological Declaration of Barmen. In effect, the League was schismatic; they knew that in order to persevere the church of Jesus Christ, they needed to break free from a church that had been infected by Naziism. Thus the Confessing Church was born.

The Confessing Church existed in Germany from 1933 to 1945. Though it gained strength in later years, it was always smaller in numbers than the Nazi-controlled German Christian Church. German pastors, more than lay people, supported the Confessing Church, and even their numbers tell a frightening story. Historian William Shirer writes, "In 1933 the 'German Christians' had some three thousand out of a total of seventeen thousand pastors. . . . Opposed to the 'German Christians' was another minority group which called itself the 'Confessional Church.' It had about the same number of pastors. . . ."[39]

What I find most interesting about those numbers is not that German Christians had as many supporters as Confessing Christians.

I am struck by the fact that if only six thousand of seventeen thousand pastors was affiliated with one of the two sides, that means that roughly eleven thousand pastors were, at least publicly, neutral. These were clergy, well-educated in Scripture and theology, who each Sunday led congregations of Christians. They were living in the shadow of an idolatrous leader and his followers, and yet they did not declare their allegiance to Christ. In fact, by 1938, most of the remaining clergy went so far as to take an oath of allegiance to Hitler himself.

Meanwhile, in 1937 alone, more than eight hundred Confessing Church pastors, including Niemöller, were arrested, with more arrests to come in the following years.[40] Niemöller spent eight months in prison before his trial, where he was found guilty but sentenced to time served. He was released, only to be rearrested by the Gestapo, who interred him in the camps at Sachsenhausen and Dachau. He was not released until the liberation of the camp by the Americans in May of 1945. (It should be noted that he was one of more than twenty-seven hundred clergy members, most of whom were Roman Catholic, who were imprisoned in the "priests' barracks" in Dachau during the war.[41])

Following the war, Niemöller wrote several versions of what has become a well-known poem. The most well-known version reads thus:

First they came for the Socialists, and I did not speak out—
Because I was not a Socialist.
Then they came for the Trade Unionists, and I did not speak
    out—
Because I was not a Trade Unionist.
Then they came for the Jews, and I did not speak out—
Because I was not a Jew.
Then they came for me—and there was no one left to speak for
    me.[42]

What Niemöller came to understand was that his own early silence made him complicit with the atrocities of the Nazi party. His eventual turn toward resistance came only after real harm had been done. By the time he became the party's target, many other voices had already been silenced. The longer it took for new members to join, the more time the Nazis party had to weaken the resistance.

In later life Niemöller would look back at his earlier stance with regret. In 1946 he wrote these words: "Thus, whenever I chance to meet a Jew known to me before, then, as a Christian, I cannot but tell him: 'Dear Friend, I stand in front of you, but we can not get together, for there is guilt between us. I have sinned and my people has sinned against thy people and against thyself.'"[43] He repented of his own early anti-Semitism and inaction. He also worked for nuclear disarmament, became immersed in peace movements, and led international ecumenical efforts through organizations like the World Council of Churches.

Until his death in 1984, Niemöller devoted himself time and again to the importance of choosing loyalty to God and God's people over false idols. When we remember him today we tend to forget his earlier acceptance of the Nazi party. It is his conversion, his turning away, from this false loyalty that must be remembered as essential to his story, though. Niemöller's life teaches us that we can indeed shift our loyalties back where they belong. Further, it shows us that we cannot choose the easier path of neutrality if we really know who and whose we are meant to be.

THE HOTTEST PLACES IN HELL

Neutrality can look so attractive. Few people enjoy conflict, and it is often easier to sit on the sidelines and wait to see how things will play out. We become apathetic, convinced we can't change anything. Or, even if we believe that we can, we tell ourselves not to get involved or to mind our own business. Neutrality is safe and comfortable.

The only problem is that when you take on the vows of baptism, whether by claiming them for yourself in the sacrament or affirming them in later life, you give up the option of neutrality. To be God's own is to give your loyalty to God alone. No longer may you choose to side with what does not bring life to others. Now you must live into that greatest commandment and love God by loving your neighbor as yourself.

President John F. Kennedy, paraphrasing Dante in a speech in Berlin in 1963, said, "The hottest places in hell are reserved for those who in a period of moral crisis maintain their neutrality."[44] I have to admit that I don't believe in hell the way that Dante did. I don't think that there's a lake of fire waiting to devour those who sin. But I do understand the sentiment. If we who have a choice do not abandon our own comfortable neutrality in order to stand for justice, we are just as guilty as the perpetrators of that injustice.

Bishop Desmond Tutu puts it this way: "If you are neutral in situations of injustice, you have chosen the side of the oppressor. If an elephant has its foot on the tail of a mouse and you say that you are neutral, the mouse will not appreciate your neutrality."[45] Having been a metaphorical mouse being stepped on by elephants at times in my life, I can tell you that is true. I never want to allow the same thing to happen to others, because I know how much it hurts.

But that's not to say that I am not sometimes tempted toward neutrality. It is a human instinct to want to keep ourselves safe. It's why we run away from burning buildings or duck when we hear loud noises. Self-preservation is important. We should never be reckless. At the same time, we should never trade our core values for a false sense of safety either. We might find that our lives can be relatively peaceful, at least for a little while, if we fade into the surroundings and stay quiet. We can make ourselves believe there's a way to follow Christ and to remain comfortable at the same time. The trouble is, if we have done our work, we know that is impossible.

In the end, loyalty to God always means loyalty to God's people, especially those who are in danger. To be a Christian means that you cannot choose silence and inaction. That is especially true if you have done the kind of self-reflective and reconciling work that we did in the first part of this book. As someone who knows that they are God's, you know that you cannot help but to act. To choose neutrality in situations that require moral courage means that you have not only been disloyal to the God who loves you, but you have chosen to be disloyal to yourself.

To resist fear, though, is to choose life. If we allow our fear to freeze us into inaction, or to allow us to run away, we pile up the stones of doubt in front of our own tombs. But if we resist we again experience a moment of resurrection. Every time we resist in order that another would be more free, we share that resurrection with them as well. In the end our loyalty only to the greatest Liberator of all will be what brings resurrection to the world.

NINE | RISKING

"IT'S NOT THE END OF THE WORLD"

In the Gospel of Matthew there's a story about Jesus talking to his disciples, trying to explain that they will face persecution and real danger. Jesus is acknowledging the threat to their lives, but he's also trying to reassure them. So he starts talking about birds, and in particular sparrows. Sparrows are a particularly odd choice because they aren't just any birds; they are especially tiny birds. You could buy two of them for a coin back then. They would seem insignificant to anyone who was listening, and utterly forgettable. And yet, Jesus tells them, if even a sparrow falls to the ground, God knows about it.

Jesus asks them, "aren't you worth more than a whole bunch of sparrows?" To put it another way, "If God is paying attention to sparrows, God is paying attention to you in this very moment" (Matt. 10:26–33, paraphrased). If something happens to a sparrow, God knows about it. So, if you, who mean more to God than many sparrows, should be in danger, wouldn't God know that too?

Jesus tells the disciples that not only does God know what is happening to each of us, but God knows the greater truths too. He tells them that the hidden things in life, everything that is unjust or causes pain or destruction, will one day be revealed. In the end the whole corrupt system is going to be exposed. Or, to quote a Johnny Cash song, Jesus is saying, "What's done in the dark will be brought to the light."[46]

Jesus is trying to put fear in perspective for his disciples. There are powerful people and systems that are threatened by Jesus's teachings, and that means that anyone who follows him is also seen as a threat to the system. The disciples are starting to understand this. They're beginning to realize that Jesus might not be leading them to a place of comfortable safety. The more this realization sinks in, the more they have to decide "What am I willing to risk?"

When the world feels wrong, when it feels like things are being done behind closed doors that will hurt us or others, it's good to be reminded that God knows those things, and that God will not let them go unexposed and unanswered. It is also good to remember that sometimes we are the ones called to do the work of confronting the injustice in our world. When we stand in the face of what is wrong, and wonder "Where is God," often the question we should be asking ourselves is "What does God want me to do about this?"

That can feel frightening, but more than that, it can make us feel hopeless. We are only one out of billions. None of us has endless assets or mighty armies at our fingertips. We may feel like we can't change things in our own neighborhoods, let alone the world. It may seem like the risk we have to take to stand up to what is wrong is more likely to backfire than to succeed.

Our lives can feel so small. The irony, though, is that we are only small if we choose to do nothing. If we instead choose to resist our fear and do what is hard, our lives become larger than we can imagine.

Jesus tells his followers that if you want to save your life, you have to lose it, and if you lose it for his sake, you will find it. It is a counter-intuitive truth, but it is true nonetheless.

In other words, if we do nothing, if we try to lay low and protect ourselves, we will lose our lives. I'm not saying that we will stop living, but I am saying that we will lose the reason that we live. We will start to lose our very souls. If we step up, though, and take the risks that Christian life calls us to take, we just might find new life. In fact, we just might thrive.

There is a story about Gene Robinson, the first openly gay bishop in the Episcopal Church. Before his consecration he received a number of threats on his life, so much so that he wore a bulletproof vest under his vestments for the ceremony. The threats continued for years, and he was frequently asked how he learned to live with them. On one occasion, when he was being interviewed on National Public Radio, he said this:

> It takes a toll. I mean, I do have to say that we made a decision early on that this is what we felt we were meant to be doing and, at some point, you have to just decide that you're going to live your life and follow what you believe God is calling you to do and let the risks take care of themselves. You know, we live in a time when if somebody wants to kill you, they're going to kill you, and you can either go in a hole and, you know, pull the roof in over you, or you just continue putting one foot in front of the other and hope that you're doing some good in the world. . . . One of the joys of being a Christian or being a person of faith is that you believe deep down that death isn't the worst thing, you know. Not living your life: that's the worst thing. And death is not, it's not all it's cracked up to be. It's not, it's not the end of the world. We actually believe that: It's not the end of the world."[47]

CHOOSING TO PARTICIPATE

The counterintuitive truth, especially for those of us who believe that we rest in the hands of an eternal and ever-loving God, is this: living a life full of fear is worse than dying. And we are all going to die. The question is, "how do you want to live?" Or, as the poet Mary Oliver writes: "Doesn't everything die at last, and too soon? Tell me, what is it you plan to do with your one wild and precious life?"[48]

There is a very good chance that the choices your faith asks you to make will not result in physical death. Your heart will likely not stop beating because you have chosen to do the right thing. But let's take this to the extreme: what if there was a chance that it would? For what, if anything, are you willing to die?

If you are like most people, that is a short list. In fact, there may be nothing on it. But think of it this way; if we are unwilling to risk our lives for all but the dearest people and ideals, why are we willing to risk our lives for our fears? Why do we allow our fear to deprive us, not of heartbeats and breaths, but of something even more precious: the fullness and beauty of a life lived well? Why are we so afraid of losing our life that we will do nothing to gain it?

In the first half of this book we undertook a journey of recovery and resurrection. We risked the kind of internal reflection and change that could bring us new life. Are we willing to now turn our backs on that new life out of fear? How can we hold on to the resurrection if we are too afraid to leave our tombs? Are we too afraid to believe that we are more than sparrows?

Think back to that picture of the man at a Nazi rally who refused to raise his arm in salute. We all want to "be that guy" and hope that we would make the right choices when our time comes. I believe that secretly we all also fear that we might not.

Truth be told, my greatest fear in life is not that I will die; it is that I will fail to have enough courage to resist fear and claim resurrection in this life. If I go to my grave having lived a comfortable and quiet existence, never taking the risks I know I should take for the good of others and the world, then I will have failed to live my faith. If I die having known recovery, and the very real resurrection it has brought, and yet I forget to respond to that grace every day of my life, then I have not really known new life.

In the prologue we talked about the three responses to fear: fight, flight, or freeze. It is "freeze" that scares me the most. I do not want to choose inaction, either because I'm too scared or too apathetic to do anything else. I don't want to mistake a complete lack of courage for appropriate caution. I want to believe in resurrection enough that my mind, body, heart, and soul are unfrozen, and I cannot help but to respond to the needs of others. This is why I was offered the resurrection of recovery—not for myself, but for others.

Some of the youth of my church taught me a new phrase several years ago during confirmation class. We were talking about bullying, and how to respond to it. They talked about how they tried to be "upstanders" and not bystanders. When they saw someone being hurt or mistreated, they wanted to be the people who did something about it, not the ones who chose to avert their eyes and keep walking. These youth did not know the literal meaning of resist: "to stand fast" or "stand again." In many ways "upstanding" and "standing fast" are the same concept. To choose to rise is to resist, and it is to participate in resurrection. To stand up to what is unjust is to resist the culture of destruction that surrounds us and to claim the resurrection anew.

THE COST OF DISCIPLESHIP

These are hopeful ideas, but they are not without risk. Dietrich Bonhoeffer was another member of the Confessing Church movement. Unlike Niemöller, Bonhoeffer did not survive imprisonment by the Nazis but was executed in April of 1945, just weeks before the end of the war.

Eight years prior to his death, what is possibly Bonhoeffer's most well-known book, *The Cost of Discipleship*, was published. In it, Bonhoeffer distinguishes between "cheap grace" and "costly grace." "Cheap grace," Bonhoeffer writes, "is grace without discipleship, grace without the cross, grace without Jesus Christ, living and incarnate.

"Costly grace," on the other hand,

> is the call of Jesus Christ at which the disciple leaves his nets and follows him. Costly grace is the gospel which must be sought again and again, the gift which must be asked for, the door at which a [person] must knock. . . . It is costly because it costs a man his life, and it is grace because it gives a man the only true life.[49]

For Bonhoeffer it was only "costly grace" that is real grace. "Cheap grace" requires nothing from us. We are not changed by it, and so it is not really from God. Costly grace, though, demands our very lives. Bonhoeffer writes, "When Christ calls a [person], he bids [them] come and die."[50] When Jesus told his disciples to take up their cross and follow him, he was talking about accepting as theirs to bear a literal instrument of death. And yet, just as Jesus says when he talks about sparrows, and just as Bonhoeffer writes, even in this we receive grace, because through this grace we receive our real lives.

Doing the right thing will almost always cost us something. In the most extreme example, we might lose our life. More likely, we will only lose the things that make our lives more comfortable. We might lose our job because we are unwilling to behave in unethical ways. We could lose our friends when we refuse to sit quietly while they tell racist jokes. Maybe we lose Facebook friends when we refuse to let bullies go unchecked. Or perhaps we risk the peace of the church when congregations decide to take a stand that is controversial.

We feel these things as losses, and that is real. But if we look closer, would any of those things really bring us life if we somehow retained them? Is a job that makes you sell your soul for money really worth it? Are friends who hurt others really friends? Is congregational peace really peace if there is no justice? In a way, isn't it grace in and of itself to lose these false promises? Could it, perhaps, even be the beginning of new life?

THE FALSE CHOICE

What both Jesus and Bonhoeffer teach us is that there is a false dichotomy between safety and the freedom to respond. When we are made to believe that our safety, or at least our quality of life, depends on our keeping quiet or remaining a bystander, we buy into a lie perpetuated by those who depend upon our complacency. The more we are willing to collude with systems that want us silent, the less true we are to who we are, and whose we are, and the more dangerous our predicament.

This is not just a theological truth. Historian Timothy Snyder, a scholar of the Holocaust and of European political extremism, wrote a short book entitled *On Tyranny*. Addressing this real dilemma, Snyder calls out those who would "trade real freedom for fake safety. . . .When [politicians] today invoke terrorism," he writes,

> they are speaking, of course, of an actual danger. But when they try to train us to surrender freedom in the name of safety, we should be on our guard. There is no necessary tradeoff between the two. Sometimes we do indeed gain one by losing the other and sometimes not. People who assure you that you can only gain security at the price of liberty usually want to deny you both.[51]

Too often we are willing to hand over our freedoms in order to serve the false idol of safety. This is especially true for Christians who, through our new life in Christ, have been freed from being held hostage to traditional ideas of safety. The greatest threat to our safety as Christians is not that we will not be safe from the real dangers of this world, but that we would be held captive by our fear of them. When that happens, when we start having more faith in our fears than in Christ, we stop being Christians.

This is hard to understand for Christians who have rarely faced persecutions. North American Christians, and our churches in particular, often worship at the altar of fear, particularly in the form of anxiety. We may know what the right thing to do is, but we are afraid of causing a stir. While peace and unity are important, they are not the mission of the church; following Jesus is our purpose. Too many churches have died, too many denominations have declined, because they refuse to take any risks in order to follow God's will for them. What use is it to hold on to what cannot save us, things like money or high membership numbers or false peace, when we stop following the One whose saving love has always surrounded us?

Christians are not called to recklessness, but we are called to respond, even in treacherous times. In Christ we are given a new kind of safety, one in which we know that God is always with us, and we are given a new freedom to respond to a world in need. Our job is not to withdraw from the world, but to engage in it. Our newspapers and news feeds will tell us where the need is and will help us understand where God is calling us next. Every time we read or hear about something we know is not right, our question to ourselves and to our churches should be, "What response does God want from us in this moment?" When we learn to ask ourselves this, and to truly discern God's will for us, we begin to find that the greatest risk we can take, the one thing that will make us lose the life we have been given, is to choose not to risk anything at all.

HOLY RISK

We are a risk-averse culture. So how do we reframe risk as a positive, and perhaps even as freedom? Think back to the Provincetown HIV survivors we talked about in chapter 7. The lives of these survivors would probably not be surprising to Malcolm Gladwell, the Canadian journalist and author whose books include *David and Goliath: Underdogs, Misfits, and the Art of Battling Giants*. Gladwell argues that underdogs, people who are not expected to persevere or succeed, are in fact often the ones most equipped to do so. Gladwell writes "we misread battles between underdogs and giants . . . we underestimate how much freedom there can be in . . . disadvantage."[52]

Many of us who have ever been seen as underdogs, who have ever been counted out, or who have been outcasts for any number of biases or other reasons know that there is a sort of odd freedom in it. In a real way, you are freed from expectations that no one should have to endure. No one believes that you will succeed, and no one can guess how you might even try to do so, and so you are given the freedom of getting to create your own path.

If you took the first half of this book seriously and embarked on your own journey of recovery, you may well identify with being an underdog made good. You know that resurrection is possible because you risked stepping into the water and crossing over from the pharoah's land to the promised land. Recovery, like resurrection, always involves a little bit of risk. Once you take that first step out of the tombs, you can never forget the freedom of fresh air and sunlight again. Daring to claim new life means you risk never being satisfied with the old one again.

If that is true, it also means that you have in a real way joined a resistance. You have decided that a life spent in the tombs is not a life at all. This is resistance to a culture of fear that teaches us to be so terrified that we never poke our heads out of the ground. To remain a part of this resistance, though, you have to be willing to risk. The good news is that if you are a person willing to do the work of recovery, like the Provincetown survivors, you have already proven to be a person willing to take a good risk. That's good news because there are some risks that are not just good, but holy.

Austrian novelist Stefan Zwieg is remembered, at least in movie form, as once stating, "Every gesture of resistance which is void of either risk or impact is nothing but a cry for recognition."[53] The bar Zwieg sets for our actions is a good one. Are we participating in displays that will change little but make ourselves feel better? Do we protest so that we can have great pictures in our social media feed, showing we were there? Or are we risking something for the good of our neighbors?

If we are willing to risk little to nothing on behalf of others, all we have done is take part in cheap resistance, and cheap resistance is the same as cheap grace. It means very little. It might make you feel better, at least for a little while, but it won't do much to help the people who really need it. If instead we are willing to risk some of what we have been given so that others might be helped, we are willing to pay a cost. This is costly grace, and this is costly resistance. This is holy risk.

Bonfoeffer wrote, "Costly grace is the Incarnation of God."[54] To go back to our story of the guy at the bottom of the hole, the one who jumps in is choosing to do so at risk to themselves. In the incarnation, God chooses a costly path, a holy risk. But it does not stop there. C. S. Lewis, drawing on the earlier thoughts of Luther and others, wrote in *Mere Christianity* what the whole purpose of our faith truly is: "The Church exists for nothing else but to draw [humans] into Christ, to make them little Christs. If they are not doing that, all the cathedrals, clergy, missions, sermons, even the Bible itself, are simply a waste of time. God became [Human] for no other purpose.[55]

If Lewis is right, and I believe he is, then our job is to be "little Christs" in this world. If Christ himself was willing to risk the worst that the world could do to him, and to jump into the hole with us, then that means we who would follow him must be willing to take risks as well. If our job is to be little Christs, that also means that resurrection must be a communal event, and we too must take part in it. The good news is that, just as Easter morning teaches us, in holy risk there can be great joy.

"I WOULDN'T BE A CHRISTIAN . . . "

Recently a good friend of mine, the Rev. Thea Racelis, wrote about her experience of being a foster parent. Recounting the advice that came to her as a first-time foster parent, she writes, "The worst advice I heard was the warning to be cautious with our love." Well-meaning friends told her things like, "You know this is risky. Be careful." They didn't want Thea and her spouse to grow attached to a child who could be taken away and returned to her birth mother. And they were right that the situation was certainly uncertain.[56]

Racelis responded to them like this: "When faced with life's many uncertainties, the answer is never going to be 'love less.' If that's the answer you come up with, you are asking the wrong questions. . . . The answer is never to love less. Love is risky." Amen. Love is indeed risky. It makes us risk the best parts of ourselves getting hurt. And yet, to not love would be even riskier; it would be to choose death, both for ourselves and for the world.

Racelis writes, "I wouldn't be a Christian if I wanted to stay safe. I will love as much and as hard as I can, for as long as I can."[57] In the end that's all that any of us who try to be Christians can do. We can love God enough to risk loving the world. We can choose love as our way of resistance, believing this holy risk to be worth it. And we can turn away from the bondage of our anxious safety, toward the costly freedom of following Christ out of the tomb and into the promise of new life.

TEN | TESTIFYING

AFTER THE TOMBS

There's a Gospel story about a man who lives, literally, among the tombs in the region of the Gerasenes. In the language of his time, he is "possessed by demons." The people in the town try to restrain him. They even bind him up with chains and put guards around him, but he is too strong. No one knows what to do, and so the man is relegated to the margins of town, where he lives naked, forced to make his home with the dead. Truth be told, a lot of people probably think he'd be better off dead, anyway (Luke 8:26–39).

And then one day, Jesus comes to town. As soon as his boat pulls ashore, the man from the tombs approaches him and, before the man can even speak, Jesus tells the demons to leave the man. Falling down and screaming, the man shouts at Jesus to go away, and not hurt him. When Jesus asks his name, he even answers back "Legion," which means many, because that's how many demons he says are inside of him.

There's a part of this story when Jesus sends the demons into a herd of pigs, which then drown themselves in the lake. It's interesting imagery, but not the point of the story. There's also the question of what the "demons" really were; likely, in twenty-first-century language, the man was suffering from a very real ailment that brought him emotional and psychological pain. The important part is that a man was suffering, and God incarnate brought him healing. The man is freed from his own demons and restored to life.

When the people from town hear of this, they don't believe it. They come out to the tombs and find that the man is dressed, awake, and completely in his right mind. So what happens next? The people from town are so amazed that they beg Jesus to stay, right? Maybe everyone believes, and decides to follow this guy? Not quite. Instead, "Then everyone gathered from the region of the Gerasenes asked Jesus to leave their area because they were overcome with fear" (Luke 8:37 CEB).

It's hard to believe, right? They had seen a man who was so tortured and sick restored to full health, and yet they were not joyful about it. They were afraid. "Overcome with fear," even. Instead of asking this Jesus to stick around, they send him packing. That's how threatening the new life he offers is to them. (And, make no mistake, that's how threatening the new life Christ offers us still is today.) So, Jesus does what they ask. He gets in the boat and leaves.

But what about the man who was in the tombs, the one whose life was just dramatically changed? He begs Jesus to let him come with him. He wants to join up as a disciple. He is ready to leave everything he knows behind and follow Jesus to the ends of the earth. Except Jesus won't let him. Jesus gives the man another mission: "Return home and tell the story of what God has done for you" (Luke 8:39). And so that's what the man does.

TELLING THE TRUTH

Had I been the man in the tombs, I might have felt frustrated with Jesus. If I had suffered so long and been pushed to the margins of my hometown, I wouldn't have wanted to stay there either. Instead, I would want to follow the one who made me whole again. That's partly about gratitude, but that's also about safety. The folks back home don't seem too friendly when it comes to people being changed, and maybe the best chance for living this new life comes somewhere out on the road, where no one knows your past.

When Jesus leaves the man behind, though, I'm convinced he knows what he is doing. Jesus may not have been welcomed in town, but he made sure someone who could tell the story remained. The man who had been healed became a reminder of God's grace and mercy. He told a story by his very survival and continued existence. He became a witness to the kind of resurrection that Christ could offer.

This language of "witness" has long been important in Christian thought. Karl Barth, of the Confessing Church's Barmen Declaration, believed that it was the task of a Christian to be a witness to Jesus Christ. In fact, the testimony of someone who is a witness to Jesus Christ, for Barth, becomes a genuine source of revelation, or of our understanding of God.[58] In other words, telling our stories of how God has changed our lives is essential to the community of faith.

So, what is testimony? Just as in the legal sense, it means to bear witness. Unlike the legal arena, though, we are not concerned with winning or losing a case, but with simply telling the truth. For Christians, this means being able to share the truth of who we understand Jesus to be and what God has done in our lives. Testimony is simply telling the story of how our life has been changed by God.

Testimony is also an important part of what it means to be in recovery. Meetings are often centered on people sharing their stories of addiction and recovery. This is sometimes referred to as "sharing our experience, strength, and hope." A speaker might share their story by talking about how their life was during addiction, what it was like to enter recovery, and how recovery informs their life now. It is always powerful to hear these testimonies, whether the person has been sober for thirty days or thirty years.

One of the unwritten rules of the recovery community is that if you are asked to share your story in a meeting, you do not say "no." The reason why is that others need to hear these stories. There may be someone in the room who is very desperate for healing and incredibly afraid that it will not come, and it may be your story that can offer a lifeline to someone on the edge. Telling our stories becomes our act of service, a testimony that can change, and even save, lives.

At the same time, telling our stories can also help us. Every time I share my story of recovery, I am reminded of the extraordinary grace I have received. I am able to understand how deadly my addiction was and how I could have destroyed my own life. In retrospect, I am also able to see where God's hand guided me and kept me safe. Each time I share, I have a chance to recommit to recovery. For this reason, I never let myself get too far away from my story.

You don't have to be in recovery, in the traditional sense, to have a story to tell. Each of us has a testimony. In the first half of the book we learned how to share it with ourselves. Here, telling our story to others becomes an act of communal faith. Keeping our stories to ourselves denies others the chance to know God's love and grace in ways to which they can relate. Sharing those stories gives others hope, it gives them assurance that things can indeed change for the better.

The main question of testimony is this: How has your life been changed by God? For the man who was in the tombs, answering this question became his purpose in life. He stayed behind, in the land of doubt, telling his town what had happened and who had made it happen. He could tell them who he had been and what he had seen. He shared his story of resurrection, and his continued testimony became a form of resurrection in and of itself.

Even those who had not seen the man's healing with their own eyes could now share in the story, and pass it on to others. Had the man not stayed in town, or had he simply stayed and remained silent, then his healing would have served only himself. Testimony became his act of hope and of service.

THE ONES WHO SPOKE FOR US

It is always the right time to tell the truth, and to share our stories, but there are times when that sharing is more crucial than ever. When injustice hits particularly close to home, or when people are suffering without hope, we must be willing to tell our truth. More than words, sharing our testimony is a concrete act of resistance. That is especially true if we have been silenced or if others are being silenced.

There's a saying attributed to George Orwell: "In a time of universal deceit, telling the truth is a revolutionary act." Those words evoke Jesus's own, which we explored earlier: "And you shall know the truth, and the truth shall set you free." In times of "universal deceit" and painful injustice, Christ's words to us ring true. Without the benefit of knowing our own story and being able to share it, we will not find freedom. The fear that makes us lock our stories away in ourselves will not save us. More importantly, it will not help anyone else either.

I am always profoundly moved by the actions of those who came out before I did, in the 1980s, '70s, '60s, and before. I know that had they not come out, had they not offered the simple yet earthshaking testimony of saying "I'm gay," I would not be able to do much of what I love in my life. I could not be married to my wife. I would not be able to serve as the pastor of a church. I might not even be alive.

This became real to me in a new way one summer about fifteen years ago. I had gone to Congressional Cemetery in Washington, DC, in order to visit the graves of my great-grandparents. Afterward I was walking back up the hill when I saw a row of graves decorated with rainbow flags, pink triangles, and a stone inscribed with the words, "Gay is good."

What I hadn't known until that day was that Congressional Cemetery is one of the only places in the world to have a gay section. But that's not the story; the story is how it came to be there. I began to understand what had happened by simply walking a few dozen yards down the row and looking at the headstone surrounded by an iron fence that bore four names. The last of those names reads: John Edgar Hoover.

J. Edgar Hoover was the founding director of the Federal Bureau of Investigation, serving from 1924 to his death in 1974. He was also staunchly antigay. During his tenure at the FBI he targeted fledgling gay rights groups for infiltration and conducted investigations into the lives of suspected "sex deviates" in government, destroying the lives of good people.[59] The fact that Hoover's own sexual orientation is a matter of debate, and that his long-time deputy director and companion, Clyde Tolson, is buried close to him, just makes the story more tragic. If Hoover was gay, his self-hatred is evident. If he was not, his fear of even being perceived as gay created terrible pain for others.

That pain is a reason why the Washington gay community chose to be buried near Hoover. Many of the graves belong to veterans and former government employees who were personally hurt by Hoover's actions. One of those veterans, Leonard Matlovich, decided to move into the neighborhood, so to speak, and purchased an adjoining plot. His headstone features two pink triangles and reads "A Gay Vietnam Veteran." Other gay leaders purchased plots in the same area.[60] Today, nearly thirty years after Matlovich's death, this corner of the cemetery remains a pocket of resistance located literally in the shadows of a memorial to a man who trafficked in fear.

It was this symbol of resistance and hope that I found as a gay twenty-five-year-old who despaired of my unequal status in my country. It is also the place where Army Captain Stephen Hill, a veteran of the Iraq War, chose to marry his husband in 2011.[61] The irony that a cemetery, a place of mourning, could become one of resistance, hope, and even joy cannot be overlooked. (After all, as I said in the prologue, the first Easter did begin in a cemetery.) When Matlovich decided to plant his small testimony within a stone's throw of one who cultivated fear, he did something that would give hope to generations of young LGBTQ people. By speaking his truth, even in death, he spoke for, and to, us all.

CREATIVITY AS RESISTANCE

I am convinced that it is in sharing stories that minds are changed. Our stories break stigmas, evoke emotion, form bonds, and increase understanding. When we listen to the stories of others and share our own, we are engaging in an act of intersectionality. This is particularly true for members of groups that have been marginalized. Sharing our stories allows us to know one another in new ways, allows us to combat entrenched biases.

The process of successfully building coalitions for change often depends on our ability to connect to one another on a human level, not a theoretical or philosophical one. There is nothing wrong with academic pursuits, but they will not be what changes minds. They will always be ancillary to the work of building interpersonal connections and creating alliances of mutual understanding and motivation.

Tyrants succeed because of their ability to split people apart. By driving a wedge between two groups that could be allied for change, they reduce the obstacles to their own pursuit of power. To choose not to be divided, but to listen instead to one another's stories, is an act of resistance. It's a refusal to let oppressive voices shape the narrative, a commitment to finding the places where our interests intersect. The bonds of understanding we form with one another by hearing these stories allow us to remain united in the faces of disinformation and the distortion of truth. The better we know the stories of others, the more we can stand up and call a lie out as a lie when our friends and neighbors are being targeted.

There are many ways we might tell our stories. Sometimes we share them as actual spoken testimonies, similar to the way one might deliver a sermon or share in a recovery meeting. Other times we have one-on-one conversations, where we both speak and listen. Our stories need not be limited by speech, though. There are other methods that are just as effective, and often even more so. There are also other ways of hearing them that have the power to change our outlook and our hearts.

The Juilliard School, perhaps the preeminent performing arts conservatory in the United States, teaches its students the concept of the "artist as citizen." The school's president, Joseph Polisi, writes, "There should be no dividing line between artistic excellence and social consciousness. America's artists of today must take on the challenge of synergistically applying these two elements if the art forms we embrace are to continue to flourish and to communicate the human values that emanate from them."[62] For Polisi, the artist is inseparable from their culture and time, and the art they create must be understood as being formed by, and speaking to, the same.

This is the reason that art is so dangerous (in the best possible way). At its best it is widely accessible, and we can experience it and be moved by it. When we go to a concert, we hear a story through the music, and we feel it in our bodies. When we view a piece of art, we see the struggle in new ways. When we attend a play or watch a movie, we can relate to characters who will change our point of view. When we read a book, we become immersed in another landscape and see the world through the eyes of the protagonist.

There is a reason why those who would oppress others are so willing to engage in censorship. They know that art is a danger to those who do not tell the truth. Everything from Michelangelo's "Last Judgment" to the Harry Potter series to Billie Holiday's "Strange Fruit" has been censored by those who were somehow threatened by the truths these works of art told and the lies they exposed. The testimonies offered by these pieces of artwork were so powerful that they had to be silenced. Of course, trying to silence the truth rarely works. As Jesus replied when he was told to quiet the people who were cheering his entrance into Jerusalem, "I tell you, if they were silent, the stones would shout!" (Luke 39–40, CEB).

Vaclav Havel, the Czech playwright, once wrote, "If the main pillar of the system is living a lie, then it is not surprising that the fundamental threat to it is living in truth."[63] As an artist he understood that unmasking the lies of the oppressors meant that they would be destabilized. This was why his own work was so heavily censored in the former Czechoslovakia and he himself was imprisoned. In the end, though, Havel became a leading figure in the "Velvet Revolution," a nonviolent overthrow of the Communist government, and later the first president of the newly reinstated Czech Republic. The artist was not just the citizen, but the leader of the citizens.

On the other side of the world, the art of resistance is also on display in South Korea. In World War II, young Korean women and girls were used by Japanese soldiers as "comfort women." They were enslaved and repeatedly sexually assaulted. In the aftermath of the war, neither official acknowledgment of these violations nor compensation has ever been given by the Japanese government. In 2011 a statue depicting a girl was installed facing the Japanese embassy in Seoul. She sits silently, staring at the embassy, offering her testimony and telling the truth in the face of silence.

There are many ways to testify, but they are all creative. Whether we are sharing our story informally or we are writing our magnum opus, we are engaging in a creative act of equal importance. Our testimony is our art, our story related to others, sent out in search of the hearts where it may connect. However we choose to tell it, whatever medium we use, we are engaging in an act of constructive citizenship and faithful involvement.

SILENCE = DEATH

However they are told, our testimonies are our resistance, and our testimonies are also our hope. During the height of the AIDS epidemic, when even the president resisted saying the name of the disease and public support for those infected was slow in coming, a group called ACT UP was formed. Standing for AIDS Coalition to Unleash Power, ACT UP sought to increase awareness of the epidemic through public actions and nonviolent civil disobedience.

ACT UP took as its motto "silence equals death." For many who were involved, that was literally true. The longer people remained silent about AIDS, the more likely they or their friends were to die. Others may have preferred for them to stay silent and complacent, but they refused. They shared their truth and their testimony, regardless of whether or not others wanted to hear it. They kept doing so until even the most reluctant ears could not ignore it. To do anything less would have been to collude with death.

When we share our testimonies, no matter how it is done, we are also proclaiming that we have hope. By rejecting the voices that want to silence us, both the external and the still very powerful ones that come from inside of ourselves, we choose to live. Silence does indeed equal death, but testimony equals life.

Martin Luther knew this when he stood before the emperor. Though the story may be embellished a little, as we saw earlier, in the end he offered his testimony. He chose to stand and to tell the truth. To choose silence, to reject the grace of God that he had come to know, would have been nothing less than spiritual death for him. The same was true for the Confessing Church. The same was true even for Leonard Maltovich, whose testimony, ironically even in death, was a rejection of silence.

Our testimonies exist for more than just us. For people of faith they exist first to tell a truth about who our God is, a truth about God's love for all. They also exist, not just for our own self-preservation and liberation, but for the good of others. Through our sharing of our testimonies we are given a chance to love our neighbors as we love ourselves.

Just as the testimonies of the gay activists buried at Congressional Cemetery gave hope to me and to other young LGBTQ folks, the testimonies we share daily can give hope to those who need it. People in recovery share testimonies knowing that they can save lives. The testimonies we offer up can help those who are facing the same situations to know that there is a way through, to realize that they have a future.

Our testimonies can also give hope to those to whom we hope to be allies. In the aftermath of Charlottesville, for instance, the willingness of white people to stand up and reject the rhetoric of white supremacy has become even more important. Our testimonies must be offered in the public square, but must also be stated plainly in more private settings. We must speak the truth at our family gatherings when a relative makes a racist comment. When someone tells an anti-Semitic joke at school or work, we have to be willing to confront it. If a friend passes on misinformation as the truth, we have to be able to trust that a true friendship allows lies to be called out.

Our silence can indeed equal death, and not just our own. It can mean literal death for our neighbors and fellow citizens. Our willingness to speak up in the face of bigotry is one measure of how willing we are to truly follow Christ. Every time we allow hateful rhetoric to go unchecked, we legitimate those ideals and provide fertile soil for them to grow. If we are unable to have a mildly uncomfortable conversation with someone we know, how can we expect to be courageous when the fruits of that soil are full grown?

Testimony is the daily act of truth telling in the face of a world that would often prefer our silence. To choose to tell our stories is to resist a culture of oppression. To create beauty through art and imagination is to defy the moral austerity of evil. To refuse to remain silent in the face of lies is to choose the path of discipleship. Testimony is nothing less than hope, for ourselves, for our neighbors, and for those to come.

We never hear what happened to the man in the tombs. After Jesus sailed off, he was left in his hometown with nothing but his testimony. Was it received? Or was his story so scary that people tried to silence him, the way they had Jesus? It's unclear. I believe that he did tell his story, though, regardless of what others said. I believe that because to truly know the grace of God, and to feel your heart changed, is an event that forever disallows your silence. When you have a testimony, you simply have to share it.

ELEVEN | DISRUPTING

TIMOTHY THE TIMID

In the early days of the church, back when Paul was preaching and teaching, there was a young man named Timothy. Timothy's mother and grandmother were Christians, and Paul was a mentor in the faith to him, a sort of spiritual father. Paul knew Timothy well and knew that he was faithful, but also timid. He was sick often, and anxious. He had stomachaches and was quiet. Paul once even wrote ahead of Timothy to the church in Corinth telling them to "put him at ease among you" (1 Cor. 16:10).

There's a sense that Timothy was someone who was more comfortable being a wallflower or working behind the scenes. Timothy traveled with Paul and helped him in his missions, a faithful assistant on the way, happy to be out of the spotlight. It wasn't long before Paul launched Timothy out on his own, though, sending him to Ephesus to build a church. For a guy like Timothy, this must have been nothing short of terrifying.

There are two letters in the New Testament that were supposedly written by Paul to Timothy, the shaky new pastor. These days scholars aren't sure whether or not Paul really wrote them. They say they could have been written by a student of Paul's who used his style. I'd like to think they really were from Paul, though, or at least from someone who knew how much Paul loved Timothy. There's something special about that because these are letters of comfort, sent out to someone who needed a boost of confidence from a mentor with a tender spirit.

"Pursue righteousness, godliness, faith, love, endurance, gentleness," Paul writes in his first letter to Timothy, encouraging him, "Fight the good fight of the faith . . . " (1 Tim. 6:11–12). Later, when Paul was in prison facing his martyrdom and it seemed uncertain that Timothy would ever see him again, another letter came. This time Paul wrote Timothy these words: "I'm reminding you to revive God's gift that is in you through the laying on of my hands. God didn't give us a spirit that is timid but one that is powerful, loving, and self-controlled. So don't be ashamed of the testimony about the Lord or of me, his prisoner. Instead, share the suffering for the good news, depending on God's power" (2 Tim. 1:6–8 CEB).

In other words, it's time to stand up and make a choice. Timothy was standing at a turning point, deciding what kind of person, and Christian, he would be. These letters came to him in that moment, reminding him of "who and whose" he was, and what that meant. Paul's reminder that "God didn't give us a spirit that is timid" was what he seemed to know Timothy needed to hear. The question was, how would Timothy respond?

HOLY RULE BREAKERS

As a child my school district gave out academic grades and conduct grades. If you were the sort of kid who never challenged the teacher, always followed the rules, and stayed out of trouble, you would get a

"1" on your report card. If you were the sort who talked incessantly and couldn't wait in lines without wandering off, you got a "2." And if, in the wake of a year with you, the teacher considered early retirement, you got a "3."

I never got anything other than a 1. I always followed the rules, no questions asked. I was the kind of well-mannered kid that teachers loved having, because I didn't challenge them and didn't cause problems. In a world where the rules were mostly for my safety and that of others, that all made sense. I didn't understand why everyone didn't just follow the rules. It made life a whole lot easier.

Then came middle school and we began studying the civil rights movement. I was still getting those "1s" on my report card, but I was beginning to understand that sometimes doing what is right requires breaking the rules. Less than thirty years before I sat in its classrooms, the very school I was attending had been segregated, and that segregation had been completely legal. The entire web of Jim Crow had been a set of rules, of racism codified into law. I began to understand that rules weren't always right.

John Lewis has talked about "good trouble" and the idea that sometimes you have to break the rules to do the right thing.[64] Lewis's history in the civil rights movement is the story of courage in action. He marched with Dr. King in Selma, spent time in Mississippi jails, and crossed the south as a Freedom Rider. Even today, as a member of Congress, he still engages in civil disobedience. In June of 2016, following the Pulse shootings in Orlando, he staged a sit-in on the floor of the House of Representatives.

John Lewis is a rule breaker and a law breaker. He is also a good man full of deep moral courage. His actions were often taken over the objections of pundits who urged him to play by the rules or use less provocative means. Lewis acted anyway, putting himself at risk and challenging unjust laws again and again. The question for those of us who would do good is how can we be more like him? How do we get over the fear of having anything less than a "1" stamped on our proverbial report card?

Malcolm Gladwell has some thoughts on this. Gladwell believes that "innovators and revolutionaries," people who want to change things for the better and who are able to produce that change, must in some way be "disagreeable." Quoting the work of psychologist Jordan Peterson, Gladwell uses what is called the "Big Five personality inventory," which defines "agreeableness" as being "cooperative/empathic versus self-interested/antagonistic." He explains why this is a good thing:

> By disagreeable, I don't mean obnoxious or unpleasant. I mean that on that fifth dimension of the Big Five personality inventory, 'agreeableness,' they tend to be on the far end of the continuum. They are people willing to take social risks—to do thing that others might disapprove of. That is not easy. Society frowns on disagreeableness. As human beings we are hardwired to seek the approval of those around us. Yet a radical and transformative thought goes nowhere without the willingness to challenge convention. "If you have a new idea, and it's disruptive, and you're agreeable, then what are you going to do with that?" says Peterson. "If you worry about hurting people's feelings and disturbing the social structure, you're not going to put you ideas forward."[65]

In other words, nice might be what society expects of us, but disagreeable is what society needs. Without people willing to push the envelopes of convention, to take social risks, progress will not happen.

Thinking back to John Lewis's story, we see a good man who is also a disagreeable man. Lewis took real risks, both social and physical. In *March,* the graphic novel–style series he co-wrote about his early life, Lewis tells the story of his own family disapproving of his actions. He remembers how he stopped coming home as often once he became active in the fight for civil rights. In some ways Lewis had to leave his family behind in order to follow his conscience. He had to be disagreeable in order to do good.[66]

We don't often like disagreement in the church. We see pursuing unity as more important than pursuing faithfulness. As we examined in part I, this kind of codependent behavior allows for dissent to be squashed and justice delayed. The appropriate anger and urgency of those who face real oppression is often dismissed, and agreeable but less-than-prophetic voices are elevated instead. The irony is that true unity is rarely achieved. We are far more often just creating the illusion of unity.

What would it mean for us to embrace the idea that sometimes we have to be disagreeable in order to follow our faith? Too often Christians believe that our calling is to just be nice. We must strive to be kind, but we must also understand what true kindness looks like. Continuing to do nothing to stop systems of oppression is not kindness, but violence. To truly love God, our neighbors, and ourselves, sometimes we have to be willing to be a little disagreeable.

And that is where we turn back to the story of Timothy.

TIMOTHY THE DISRUPTER

When Timothy received his letters from Paul, he was deciding what kind of Christian he was going to be. I think Paul knew that, and was writing to him, praying that he would remember who he was and trust in the Holy Spirit enough to make the right choices. Paul knew now was the time for Timothy to stop being timid and start being bold. In order to follow the gospel to all the places he needed to go, the shy and good young man had to learn how to be just a little disagreeable sometimes.

There are stories about the rest of his life that tell us that Timothy did just that. Timothy lived to the age of about eighty, a good long life back then, and he became a witness to God's love and to the gospel of Jesus Christ. He was the bishop of Ephesus, and he took some un-popular stands against the pagan worship practices of the day. One day he stood in front of a procession in honor of the goddess Diana and blocked the path of the crowd that was carrying a large idol. They were so angry with him that they beat him, dragged him through the streets, and killed him. Timothy became a martyr for the faith.

We might hear that and think, "Just let them have their parade . . . don't die for it." We might even think that Timothy should not have disrupted the religious practices of others. Indeed, if you came across the modern-day parade of another religious faith today, I'd agree. Just step to the side, and let them pass. That's why we have to understand that we are reading these two-thousand-year-old stories with twenty-first-century eyes, and we have to put those same stories in context.

Instead of thinking of the procession as a show of faith, think of it as a show of power and idolatry. Think of the things that culture makes an idol: money, war, power. Think of the social ills those things create: greed, violence, hatred, and xenophobia. And now think of standing in front of them and saying that they are not going to rule this world anymore. That's the work of those who would follow Christ. It is to face down everything that keeps this earth from being as it is in heaven; it is to be courageous, even when we want to be timid. Some-times we must dare to be disagreeable when it would be easier to just go along with things. To acquiesce might indeed be easier, but we know that it won't be right.

Timothy was a disrupter. He literally disrupted a crowd. The Latin root of the word "disrupt" means "to break apart or split," and that was what Timothy was trying to do. He wanted the crowd to break away from their worship of false idols, to split from their false alle-giances. The same root has another meaning, though, one that speaks to the task of faith, and that is to "burst" or "break open."

God bursts into our lives in disrupting ways. We are not broken down by this (though it may feel like it at the time) but rather "broken open." We become open to God and to our neighbors, and more open to change. When God breaks into our communities of faith the same thing happens. Our peace and quiet becomes disrupted, and we become compelled to act. Is it a surprise that the same God who disrupts our own lives might ask also us to also disrupt the world a little? Is it such a surprise that maybe God wants us to engage in a little of John Lewis's brand of "good trouble"?

If Timothy is any indication, it shouldn't be a surprise at all.

RUINING THANKSGIVING DINNER

In the aftermath of the August 2017 white supremacist rally in Charlottesville, Virginia, my town held a vigil. We stood with candles in front of the town hall and pledged that we would not be silent in the face of neo-Nazi rhetoric. It was a beautiful and heartening night. As we were leaving, a young girl, no older than eight, came up to me.

"Excuse me," she said, "What are we going to do now?"

The question shook me. We, a crowd of middle-class and upper-middle-class people, at least 95 percent of us white, had taken a good first step. We had refused to turn our heads the other way when the images of hate and violence had filled our screens. But what now? How could we actually disrupt the racism, anti-Semitism, and pure evil we had seen on display the night before?

Bending down, I explained, in as age-appropriate a way as possible, that now we had to keep working. We had to build a town where our friends and neighbors would always be safe and loved. We had to learn to tell the truth when people were hateful. She looked at me with confusion and said, "No, I mean, what are we doing right now? Are we all going home, or going to do something else?"

I laughed at my earnestness, but her first question stuck with me. "What are we going to do now?" It's good to show up to vigils, but it's too easy to simply do that and feel like you've done enough. In the days after Charlottesville, though, I came up with an answer. What are we going to do now? We're going to ruin Thanksgiving dinner.

I don't mean that literally, unless of course your family's Thanksgiving dinner needs a little ruining. What I'm imagining, though, are all those places where we hear something said that is hateful or ignorant or dangerous, things that make us uncomfortable, but things we don't address because we have the privilege of staying silent. I'm talking about moments like when your racist uncle makes a casual anti-Semitic joke and then in the next breath asks for the mashed potatoes. You sit there, wanting to say something but knowing that, if you do, Thanksgiving dinner will become an all-out argument. In short, you choose to keep a false peace rather than disrupt it.

Maybe it's not Thanksgiving dinner for you. Maybe it's your co-worker who passes on misinformation, sharing shocking-sounding stories about the danger of immigrants. You don't want work to be weird, so you just ignore it. Or it could be your friend who makes a comment about a woman that you just know isn't right, but you like him and so you make excuses for him instead of calling him out.

Each of us carries certain privilege that allows us to enter comfortably into certain spaces. It might be white privilege, or male privilege, straight privilege, Christian privilege, class privilege, or any number of other things. We often enjoy the comfort of those spaces so much that we choose not to be disrupters when we should be. Those are the times, though, when our voice matters the most. When we hear something hateful or untrue about a group of people who are not represented in the room, it is our job as people of faith to disrupt it, to tell the truth. It may make us uncomfortable, and it may make others uncomfortable, but our momentary discomfort is nothing compared to the very real fear that others feel every day.

Every time we do this, we disrupt the soil before the seeds of hatred and intolerance can be planted. By stopping them early, we keep them from taking root and growing into the kind of weeds that choke the life out of anything they touch. Every time we fail to do this, we may as well be standing by with a hose, ready to water those seeds ourselves. It is far better to break things open before any of that can happen.

We spent the last chapter talking about testimony. In many ways, our willingness to disrupt is correlated to our willingness to testify. Disruption is a form of telling our stories, and a way of telling the truth. In the first part of this book we learned how to tell our stories to ourselves. In the last chapter we talked about learning to tell our truth to others. In disruption we learn how to tell the truth about unjust systems and to resist unjust systems. That truth can be disruptive, and we can seem disagreeable in the telling, but it is ultimately a form of testimony, a sign that our ultimate allegiance is to a God who teaches us to love our neighbors more than our own comfort.

If that means that sometimes we have to ruin Thanksgiving dinner, then that's okay. Some people were never invited to the table anyway.

EVERYTHING WAS LEGAL . . .

But what about those moments that come in places far more public than a dining room table? In April of 1963, eight white clergymen in Alabama wrote an open letter aimed at supporters of the civil rights movement. Worried about the Rev. Dr. Martin Luther King's plans to come to Birmingham and hold public demonstrations against Jim Crow laws, they asked King to delay the protests and encouraged his supporters to disengage. They wrote that in terms of righting these injustices, "proper channels" must be used.

They concluded: "We further strongly urge our own Negro community to withdraw support from these demonstrations and to unite locally in working peacefully for a better Birmingham. When rights are consistently denied, a cause should be pressed in the courts and in negotiations with local leaders, and not in the streets. We appeal to both our white and Negro citizenry to observe the principles of law and order and common sense."[67]

The eight men who wrote that letter were not bad people. On the question of civil rights, they were moderate to liberal Catholic, Jewish, and Protestant clergy. Many supported Dr. King's ideals, if not his tactics. They were not, however, disrupters—at least in this situation. Whatever fears they had about how the marches would go outweighed the respective faiths they proclaimed. In their day, though, many agreed with them and supported their idea of slower, less confrontational methods.

It is not their letter that we best remember, but the one written by Dr. King four days later from his cell in the Birmingham city jail. Addressing them, he writes,

> We know through painful experience that freedom is never voluntarily given by the oppressor; it must be demanded by the oppressed. Frankly, I have yet to engage in a direct action campaign that was "well timed" in the view of those who have not suffered unduly from the disease of segregation. For years now I have heard the word "Wait!" It rings in the ear of every Negro with piercing familiarity. This "wait" has almost always meant "Never." We must come to see, with one of our distinguished jurists, that "justice too long delayed is justice denied."[68]

For King, the time for disruption had long since passed, and appeals to "law and order and common sense" were tantamount to siding with the oppressor. Reminding them of the difference between what is legal and what is ethical, he writes further down the page, "We should never forget that everything Adolf Hitler did in Germany was 'legal' and everything the Hungarian freedom fighters did in Hungary was 'illegal.' It was 'illegal' to aid and comfort a Jew in Hitler's Germany. Even so, I am sure that, had I lived in Germany at the time, I would have aided and comforted my Jewish brothers."[69]

I am far from an anarchist. Inside I'm still the kid who got all 1s in conduct. I believe, nevertheless, that the example of men like Timothy, King, and Lewis cannot be ignored. There are simply some moments when following Jesus means standing up to unjust laws and systems. As King said, what the Third Reich did was indeed allowed under the laws they set up. In their own reign, they could be convicted by no court. They were not only following the law, but upholding it.

For a Christian, though, loving our neighbors means answering to a higher law. Christian ethics demand that we do what is good, and they also demand that we refuse to call what is unjust "good." God's call to us must disrupt our allegiance to all that is unjust. To truly move beyond idolatry means being willing to follow Christ, even when it means breaking the rules as we know them. This must always be done in discernment, both with God and with a community, for it cannot be taken lightly. But in the moments when God's call to us is in conflict with the lines drawn by others, we must know which voice we will obey.

DISAGREEABLE DISRUPTERS

The task for Christians, particularly those of us who have the privilege of not being under attack in a given situation, is to learn how to be bold enough to be disagreeable disrupters from time to time. A faith that makes us apathetic and uninterested is no faith at all. Following Christ means sometimes being unpopular. It also means that sometimes we will end up paying a price for our disruption. Living into our faith means knowing that those are small matters compared to the saving disruption of the love of Christ.

Jesus was a "disagreeable disrupter" himself. He crossed barriers and broke human rules, all in service to God's greater standard. He angered religious authorities and civil leaders, and he flipped over tables in the Temple. No one could call Jesus overly concerned with whether or not people liked him. Beyond that, Jesus's very life and resurrection was a disruption to the forces of destruction.

If we are supposed to be "little Christs" to one another, as C. S. Lewis said, then that means sometimes we are called to be disagreeable disrupters as well. We are called to take our worth not from what others think about us, but from God. Our marching orders come not from our desire to please others, but a desire to follow Jesus. The irony in that is that by following Jesus, by choosing to sometimes be disagreeable or disruptive, we are not abandoning humanity or dismissing them as unimportant. Instead, we are working to better love one another by learning from the priorities of the one who loved us first.

In Christ's life we learn that love disrupts even death. Christ's call to us to love God, self, and neighbor is a radical disruption of the way things too often go. We are called back, and called into disagreement with the idols of this world. We are called to follow Christ, called to participate in the building of a better way. Disruption is resistance to all that keeps this world from being as God intends it. When done with discernment and integrity, disruption is a key step in our participation in the renewal of creation.

T W E L V E | R E F O R M I N G

DIVING IN

So many of the best stories in the Bible take place around water. I think there's something significant about that. Norman Mclean, the American writer whose books include *A River Runs Through It,* once wrote "stories of life are often more like rivers than books."[70] The stories of life are like rivers, and they are like oceans, too, and like the seas where pilgrims wade in and disciples sail. Wherever there is water there is depth and danger. And wherever there is water, there is hope.

When Nachshon stood on the banks of the Red Sea, trembling before it, he made the choice to get in and to risk everything for new life. When we enter the waters of baptism, we enter a covenant in which all else is subject to the vows that we have made to Christ. In the hopeful metaphors of Revelation, we are told that there is a "river of the water of life, bright as crystal, flowing from the throne of God and of the Lamb through the middle of the street of the city" (Rev. 22:1–2).

Many of the disciples were fishermen. They spent their lives on the water, and the water gave them life and livelihood. Their occupation means that they also knew the dangers that were just below the surface. Like all of us, their instinct was to stay safe. Perhaps that's why the story of Jesus walking on water is so compelling.

The story begins with the disciples out on the water in a boat together. They are by themselves, and Jesus is back on the shore praying. Halfway across the water they look out and see something coming toward them. At first they think it's a ghost, which is fair because that's probably more logical than what it really was. Somehow, Jesus was walking on water and coming to them.

Jesus yells to them, "Don't be afraid . . . it's me." And Peter, who is just so earnest in times like this, says to him, "Jesus, if it's really you, tell me to walk on the water over to you." So Jesus says, "come on." And Peter does it. He starts walking on water too. He even makes it a few steps, but then he seems to realize what he is doing. Suddenly a strong wind picks up all around him, and he panics.

Peter falls into the water, and starts to sink, calling out for Jesus to help him. Jesus pulls him up, and says to him, "You of little faith . . . why did you doubt?" It isn't until Jesus gets him back to the boat, and the wind dies down, that the disciples start to understand, just a little more clearly, that Jesus is more than he seems (Matt. 14:22–33).

I've read this story so many times over the years, and I've always thought that it was a cautionary tale about Peter, how he didn't have enough faith. If only Peter had not doubted, then he wouldn't have panicked when he saw that he was walking on water. I figured it was a message to us all: if you just believe enough, you can do the things that you've never imagined, things like walking on water.

Recently I've begun to wonder if the point isn't that Peter could have walked on water had he been more faithful. Maybe, just maybe, the point is that if Peter had found a little more faith, he wouldn't have been so scared of going into those waters. Maybe, had he not doubted that Jesus would be there with him, he would have even been ready to go in.

I say that because, more and more, I think the point of being a Christian is not to stay safe and dry. I think following Christ means getting out of our boat, and diving in, unafraid of the deep waters and what lies beneath. Peter wants to walk on water. He wants to do something special, something others can't, something that keeps him above the unknown abyss. Peter wants Jesus to do something for him, and to give him this power. But the point of being a Christian is not getting something from Jesus. The point is to follow Jesus wherever he goes, even into the deepest waters.

I often struggle with the temptation of staying in the boat when the seas get choppy. On my best days, I might even dare to try walking on water, staying safely above the fray. Metaphorically, I have enough privilege to do that. I can venture from the safety of my boat, take a few unsure steps, and jump back in before I sink down into the waves.

But really, walking on water is just a party trick. It's a sort of performance. We think that walking on water is impressive. It's not. Walking on water is nothing to aspire to. It's just one more way to avoid the real work. Instead, we have to be willing to risk jumping in, diving to face what scares us. We have to learn to trust that even in the deep waters—especially in the deep waters—God will be with us, making sure we do not drown.

I refuse to try to walk on water anymore, staying safe and dry. Instead, I'm ready to plunge into the waters of my baptism and to resist evil and oppression in every form. I was not baptized into safety. I was not baptized to stay in the boat. I was baptized into a life of following a Savior who calls us out of silence and apathy and into the deep end, so that we might tell the truth and love our neighbors as ourselves.

In this last chapter we will explore what it means to participate in the work of creation and re-creation. We will follow the path of those who have come before us who have turned their disruption into an act of reformation. Just as the work from part I of this book is never-ending, so is the work to come. Having journeyed until this point, we are prepared for what lies ahead. We are diving into the work of re-forming, and re-forming, the world with God. The waters may be deep and intimidating, but we do not enter them alone.

FORMING AGAIN

In the waters of creation God brought beauty and order out of chaos and created new life. In the waters of our baptism we commit to working with God to restore humanity and creation to God's vision for us. The Creator made this world, and all who dwell in it, "very good" (Gen. 1:31). When what was "very good" meets with injustice, oppression, or evil, though, the Creator's vision becomes obscured.

We began this book by talking about recovery. That may have seemed an odd place to start for a book about resistance, but in recovery we learn that nothing, and no one, is beyond redemption. It is never too late for recovery, in every sense of the word. Learning to do the work of recovery in ourselves was the first part of learning how to facilitate recovery in the larger world. If God gave all things their form and called these things "very good," recovery is the work of helping ourselves, our neighbors, and our world to remember—to recover—that goodness.

That does not mean that we impose our Christian worldview on them, but that we work from that worldview to affirm the worth and dignity of others. We work to help recovery happen wherever it needs to take place, whether in our hometowns or across the world. We respect the agency of others, and we ask how we can help, always ready to lend our hands to the work of recovery yet to be done.

In this journey we will discover something important: recovery is just another way of saying "reformation." To "reform" something is literally to "re-form" it. We help to form it again. Whether that is the reformation of ourselves, as we follow a plan of recovery, or the reformation of our communities and world, we are taking what is good, but has grown broken and distorted, and helping it to find that goodness once again.

The reality of living in this world is that we are going to forget "who and whose" we are. The image of God that we have been created in will be distorted by the brokenness of the world. The reality of sin, and of sinful systems, will confuse us and lead us away from what is holy. We will get it wrong, even when we try to get it right. We will hurt ourselves, and one another, even when we don't want to.

If we are faithful, though, we will dare to jump into the chaos, whether inside of ourselves or in the world, and do our best to help to re-form what we see. We will work to bring things not back to the way they used to be, but into a future where God's love and grace is felt more deeply every day. In the reality of chaos we will find, not an occasion for anarchy, but an opportunity for hopeful creativity.

We are called to be re-formers in our own lives, and in our communities. We are called to take apart systems of destruction and oppression and re-form them into that which gives life. We are called to break the hold of evil and replace it with the power of grace and forgiveness. We are called to work hard, and we are to be creative and imaginative. We must protest, but we cannot stop there. We must be willing to go deeper than surface level, to dare to build something new. This is going to be hard work that challenges us daily—work that we will never finish in this lifetime.

The good news is that our partner in this creativity, the master artist, is the Creator. God is ultimately in control, but we are called to assist in this work. We are called to recover God's vision for us and to re-form the broken creation into something new. By our very participation we resist because, when we dare to enter into this partnership, we proclaim that we have hope for the world. To believe that re-formation is possible, to believe in the power of recovery, is to proclaim that God's love and grace will have the last word.

THE REFORMATION, CONTINUED

Make no mistake, though, doing things a new way is rarely easy. Recently the town where I live made a decision to take out a centuries-old dam that sat on the river that runs through town. The earliest version of the dam had been placed there by the first European immigrants who arrived in this area, back in 1647. It had supplied mills with their power for centuries and had been a part of the landscape for generations. It was beautiful to look at, too. The water poured over the edge of the dam and rushed down into town.

The only trouble was that we don't have mills here anymore. Nothing is being manufactured downtown, so no jobs depend on it. At the same time the alewives, saltwater fish that have used this brackish river to spawn for at lot longer than the mill has been around, were beginning to suffer. This was concerning because when one piece of the ecosystem dies off, the rest follows. The dam, which no longer served a purpose, was negatively affecting the sustainability of the whole river and the entire watershed that it fed.

The town made a decision to remove the dam. A vote was taken and work began. Before long the dam was gone, and we all waited with anticipation for the waters to roar again. Except they didn't. Day after day we would go to the river, look down, and see a dusty riverbed with small pockets of water. Everyone in town began to wonder if we'd made a big mistake. Maybe that old, historic dam wasn't so bad?

When we try something new, it can be anxiety producing. Reformation is often slow, and the results can be hard to see. We can get discouraged pretty easily and start doubting ourselves. Often we begin to wonder if things weren't better off before all this so-called progress. Maybe we should just go back to the way things always were. Was it really so bad back then?

If you work for progress, you will see this kind of doubt and discouragement more than once. It's never easy. Even after Moses got the people over the Red Sea, they still wandered in the wilderness for forty years questioning what in the world he was doing. They even found themselves wondering the unthinkable: "Maybe things would have been better back in Egypt, back when we were slaves."

But going backwards isn't an option. Regression will never save us. Continued reformation is the only option that comes with life. As people of faith, we know this. Christian faith is inherently "progressive"; we are people who always move forward, progressing toward God and the future that God is preparing for us, and not away.

Protestant Christians are sometimes referred to as "people of the Reformation." The idea that even something as holy as the church must be reformed is in our very lifeblood. (Catholics and Orthodox Christians know this too, and their own traditions have had their own times of reformation.) The Reformation that began five hundred years ago was an act of recovery. The reformers believed themselves to be recovering the original goodness of Christ's church and re-forming the church in that image.

Too often we believe that the Reformation ended with them. The reality is that reformation continues today. The Reformed tradition has a phrase that describes this: *Ecclesia reformata, semper reformanda.* That translates to "the church reformed and always being reformed." The process of becoming is never done. The church is being made more perfect in each generation.

The same can be true of this world, if we dare to imagine something different and to work toward re-formation. Reformation becomes resistance in action, a refusal to regress or to remain apathetic about the present. Participating in the continued reformation of ourselves and our world is refusing to accept that we are ultimately powerless. To dare to reform is to dare to be alive.

It is this truth that reminds me that "resistance" is not a buzzword. It is not something that became trendy in recent years. It is a struggle against apathy and repression that is as old as humanity. It is what brought Jesus out of the grave, Luther to the doors of the Wittenberg church, and Dr. King across the Selma bridge. Resistance will not be a short-lived period of heightened activity. If we are done resisting in a few years, then we were never part of the resistance anyway. Resistance is a lifelong journey of daring to re-form. And it is a task that one day we will hand off to the next generation.

TRUE GENERATIVITY

We watched the river in my town for weeks, certain that the water would never come. Then one day it rained. The riverbed filled, and the waters flowed. The upper river connected again with the lower, and the current rushed as it never had before. In the late days of the spring I stand on the bridge just below where the dam had been. Looking down I watch the alewives fighting their way up the current, going back to the waters of their own creation, beginning the cycle again for a next generation.

Reformation never ends with us, and resistance is never just for our own sake. To go back to Erik Erikson's idea of "generativity," it really is about what we do to create something for the ones who come after us. If we want a world for them that is "very good," the steps toward the recovery of that goodness that we take now will show our care for them. In a real way, we are removing the dams that block the way for the living water to flow.

Our work as Christians always includes equipping the next generation to live out our faith. Christians are called to lives of resistance, which means that we must teach those coming after us what it means to resist. How we live in these times will provide an example for them. The ways we engage with the world, transforming systems of oppression into systems of love and justice, will teach them more surely than anything else how to be Christians.

The challenge facing the church in these days is to refuse to collude with systems of oppression. It is to dive into our baptismal waters rather than stay in silence and safety in the boat. The age of compulsory American Christianity is over, and with it the time for silence and neutrality. We must stop worrying about the consequences of rocking the boat and start worrying about getting out of a boat that is taking us nowhere fast.

The next generation will not remain in that boat, regardless of whether or not we do. They are already jumping in, ahead of us. They can jump with the knowledge of "who and whose" they are, or they can jump without it. Either way, they will not stay put. What would it mean for the church to decide "We're going to jump with them"?

And what would it mean to make the commitment to the next generation after that to make sure that they are mentored, educated, and equipped in their faith? If we take seriously the duty of being generative and reject the option of stagnating in apathy, we can re-form the church into a place of hopeful resistance. We can become a place where we are not just allowed but encouraged to live out our baptismal vows with courage and faith.

We will not do this just for the next generation but also for one another. Every time we learn to stand up in the face of what is not right, we empower others to do the same. The first person in a room who is willing to speak words of challenge or dissent, who dares to proclaim another way, enables others who might otherwise say nothing. The first to find the courage to act against injustice inspires others to find their own courage. The first candle that is lit is able to provide light to a host of others, stopping only when that light is no longer passed on.

There is a sign on the wall of my office that reads "Be who you needed when you were younger." When I saw it in the store, it stopped me in my tracks. The reality of life is that none of us gets exactly what we need all of the time. Can you imagine, though, how your life might have been different had you had the understanding, support, and encouragement you needed? How could you have resisted fear and found courage if you had seen someone like yourself, fully embodied and living with integrity in the world? What choices would you have dared to make if you knew that being faithful meant being bold?

How could the life of the next generation, or even our own, be made better if we were willing to jump in the hole with them and tell them, "I was here before, and I know the way out"?

We are people of faith who believe in the power of resurrection. We believe that new life is possible, which means that means we believe in the power of recovery and reformation. If we dare to resist the fear that holds us back then, with just a little bit of courage, we will find that the deepest waters are no match for our faith and the darkest tombs will not contain us. Reformation is an act of hope for the future. It is resistance with the will to build something better. It is our gift to the world to come.

THE NEXT RIGHT STEP

We are coming to the end of our journey, or at least this part of it. We have traveled through a process of recovery to one of resistance, and in the end we have discovered that in many ways they are the same. We are always being re-formed by God, and we are always called to participate in the work of re-forming our world.

In the end the point of this work is love. Love is the ultimate resistance to the worst that this world can do. Recall that when Jesus was asked the greatest commandment he said this: " 'You shall love the Lord your God with all your heart, and with all your soul, and with all your mind.' This is the greatest and first commandment. And a second is like it: 'You shall love your neighbor as yourself' " (Matt. 22:37–39).

The love of God, self, and neighbor is where it all begins and ends. We cannot have any of the others without having them all. The person who cannot love themselves cannot love their neighbors. The person who cannot love their neighbors cannot love God. And the person who cannot love something greater than themselves cannot love anything.

When we began this journey we were standing with Nachshon at the edge of the Red Sea, with the pharoah's horsemen closing in, deciding whether or not we dared to take the next step. Even all these pages later, we are still thinking about our next step. That is because we are always there. We are always standing, looking out at the waters, and deciding whether or not we dare to move forward.

The truth is that we don't just cross the Red Sea once. We cross it again and again in our lives, each time summoning up the courage to immerse ourselves in its waters. Every day we make the choice to keep moving and to keep recovering the image of God in us all.

In midrashic tradition it is taught that the Red Sea did not part completely for Nachshon, even when he waded in until the waters were at his head. Instead, a small portion opened. Again and again, Nachshon had to dare to step forward, and, step by step, the path was revealed. He never was able to stand on the shore and see his way to the other side.

In recovery we have a saying: just do the next right thing. I think Nachshon would have appreciated that. In the end all we have to do is resist our fear and ask God to give us the courage to do the next right thing, to take the next right step, trusting that God will stick with us every inch of the journey. I trust in that, because this is the same God who loved us enough to jump in the hole with us and show us the way out.

As we move forward through our own waters of challenge, we must choose our own next right steps. And so, as we do, the greatest commandment becomes our guide, even in the scariest of currents. When you are unsure, remember this: if the next step you take is done in love—love of God, love of yourself, and love of your neighbor—it will always be the right one.

This is the point of faith: take each step with love. Recover the goodness of God that exists in you and all of creation. Re-form the things that you can. And resist the fear that holds you back from being exactly who and whose you are meant to be.

As you dare to enter these waters, may God's grace and love surround you every day, and may you find courage in every step.

Notes

PROLOGUE: IN THE TOMBS

1. *The West Wing*, episode 32, "Noël," teleplay Aaron Sorkin, story Peter Parnell, broadcast December 20, 2000.

2. More about Erikson's theories can be found in his *Identity and the Life Cycle* (New York: W. W. Norton, 1994).

3. For more on this, see my first book, *Glorify: Reclaiming the Heart of Progressive Christianity* (Cleveland: Pilgrim Press, 2016).

4. Robert Pazmino, "Teaching Both Who and Whose We Are: Honoring Individuality and Connection." *Christian Education Journal* 11/2 (Fall 2014):421–28.

CHAPTER ONE: READY

5. J. K. Rowling, *Very Good Lives* (New York: Little, Brown, 2015), 33.

6. See the Book of Jonah.

7. For many people in recovery our Higher Power is God. That is true for me and, if you are reading this book, likely also true for you. I will use the language of God here while also acknowledging that others hold different concepts of their Higher Power.

8. Edited for inclusivity.

CHAPTER TWO: HONEST

9. Jerome Hunt, "Why the Gay and Transgender Population Experiences Higher Rates of Substance Use," March 9, 2012, Center for American Progress.

10. Richard Brouilleette, "Why Therapists Should Talk Politics," *New York Times*, March 15, 2016.

11. Ibid.

12. Dietrich Bonhoeffer, *The Cost of Discipleship* (New York: Simon & Schuster/Touchstone, 1995), 110.

13. John Calvin, *Institutes of the Christian Religion* (Peabody, MA: Hendrickson, 2008), 4.

CHAPTER THREE: RECONCILED

14. Alcoholics Anonymous, *The Big Book, 4th ed.* (Alcoholics Anonymous World Services, 2001), 83–84.

15. Henri Nouwen, *The Return of the Prodigal Son* (New York: Doubleday, 1994), 117.

CHAPTER FOUR: WHOLE

16. Bonhoeffer, *Cost of Discipleship*, 48.

17. Bonhoeffer's *Cost of Discipleship* gives a classic explanation of "cheap grace" and "the cost of discipleship."

18. William Sloane Coffin, "Limitations," sermon, July 5, 1981.

19. e. e. cummings, "A Poet's Advice to Students," in e. e. cummings, *A Miscellany*, ed. George Firmage (New York: Argophyle, 1958), 13.

20. Susan Cain, *Quiet: The Power of Introverts in a World That Can't Stop Talking* (New York: Random House, 2013), 21.

CHAPTER FIVE: CONNECTED

21. Episcopal Diocese of Maryland, "Heather Cook Case: Timeline of Events," http://latestnews.episcopalmaryland.org/wp-content/uploads/2015/02/TIMELINE.Updated.2.10.15.pdf.

22. Al-Anon is the twelve-step fellowship for family and friends of alcoholics and addicts that helps members to learn how not to enable their loved ones.

23. Carol Glatz, "Pope Francis: Devil prefers comfy, business-savvy church that overlooks truth, *America* magazine, May 23, 2017.

24. Tradition 2 of AA.

CHAPTER SIX: INVESTED

25. Bonhoeffer, *Cost of Discipleship*, 38.

26. Edited for inclusivity.

27. UC Davis Health, "Gratitude is good medicine," Nov. 5, 2015, https://www.ucdmc.ucdavis.edu/welcome/features/2015-2016/11/20151125_gratitude.html.

28. Ibid.

29. Erikson, *Identity and the Life Cycle*, 103.

30. Ibid.

CHAPTER SEVEN: PERSEVERING

31. Heiko A. Oberman, *Luther: Man Between God and the Devil*, transl. Eileen Walliser-Schwarzbart (New Haven, CT: Yale University Press, 2006), 39.

32. John Calvin, *Institutes of the Christian Religion*, John T. McNeill, transl., Library of Christian Classics (Philadelphia: Westminster, 1960), 689, edited for inclusivity.

33. cummings, "A Poet's Advice."

34. Margaret Cho, *I Have Chosen to Stay and Fight* (New York: Riverhead Books, 2005).

35. Alice Walker, *Possessing the Secret of Joy* (New York: Simon & Schuster, 1992).

36. *Watermark,* June 16, 2016.

CHAPTER EIGHT: CHOOSING

37. *Book of Confessions: The Constitution of the Presbyterian Church* (USA), "The Theological Declaration of Barmen," 8.03.

38. Ibid., 8.07, 8.08, 8.10–8.28.

39. William Shirer, *The Rise and Fall of the Third Reich* (New York: Simon & Schuster, 1987), 235–36.

40. Ibid., 239.

41. John Vidmar, *The Catholic Church through the Ages* (Mahwah, NJ: Paulist Press, 2005), 329.

42. United States Holocaust Memorial Museum, Washington, DC.

43. United States Holocaust Memorial Museum, quoting from Niemöller's book *Of Guilt and Hope* (New York: Philosophical Library, 1947).

44 National Archives, *Public Papers of the Presidents of the United States: John F. Kennedy,* 1963, p. 503.

45. Gary Younge, "The Secrets of a Peacemaker," *The Guardian,* 22 May 2009.

CHAPTER NINE: RISKING

46. Johnny Cash, "God's Gonna Cut You Down," on *American V: A Hundred Highways* 2006 (posthumously), American Recordings/Lost Highway Records.

47. Interview, *Fresh Air,* NPR, January 10, 2013.

48. Mary Oliver, "The Summer Day," in *New and Selected Poems* (Boston: Beacon Press, 1992), 94.

49. Bonhoeffer, *Cost of Discipleship* (edited for inclusivity), 45.

50. Ibid, 89.

51. Timothy Snyder, *On Tyranny: Twenty Lessons from the Twentieth Century* (New York: Random House, 2017), 99–100.

52. Malcolm Gladwell, *David and Goliath: Underdogs, Misfits, and the Art of Battling Giants* (New York: Little, Brown, 2013), 93.

53. Glenn Kenny, "Review: 'Stefan Zweig: Farewell to Europe,' Hello to Exile," *New York Times,* May 10, 2017.

54. Bonhoeffer, *Cost of Discipleship,* 45.

55. C. S. Lewis, *Mere Christianity* (New York: HarperOne, 2015), 199–200, edited for inclusivity.

56. Thea Racelis, "Why I Can't Be Cautious with My Love," blog post on New Sacred: A United Church of Christ Blog, May 19, 2017.

57. Ibid.

CHAPTER TEN: TESTIFYING

58. *Time* magazine, cover story, "Witness to an Ancient Truth, April 20, 1962.

59. Dudley Clendinen, "J. Edgar Hoover, 'Sex Deviates' and My Godfather," *New York Times,* Nov. 25, 2011.

60. Ella Morton, "The Only LGBT Cemetery Section in the World Was Inspired by J. Edgar Hoover," *Atlas Obscura,* March 30, 2016.

61. Story of His Stone, http://www.leonardmatlovich.com/story ofhisstone.html.

62. Joseph Polisi, *The Artist as Citizen* (Pompton Plains, NJ: Amadeus Press, 2005), 11.

63. Snyder, *On Tyranny,* 77–78.

CHAPTER ELEVEN: DISRUPTING

64. Katie Mettler, "Good Trouble: How John Lewis fuses new and old tactics to teach about civil disobedience," *Washington Post,* June 16, 2016.

65. Gladwell, *David and Goliath*, 115–17.

66. John Lewis and Andrew Aydin, *March*, illus. Nate Powell (Marietta, GA: Top Shelf Productions, 2013–16).

67. Statement by Alabama Clergymen, April 12, 1963, © Estate of Martin Luther King Jr, reprinted by the American Friends Service Committee.

68. Martin Luther King Jr., "Letter from a Birmingham Jail," April 16, 1963, in *Why We Can't Wait* (New York: Harper & Row, 1964).

69. Ibid.

CHAPTER TWELVE: REFORMING

70. Norman McKlean, *A River Runs Through It* (Chicago: University of Chicago Press, 1989), 63.